LAWS OF LOVE SET IN STONE

J . JOHN

David C Cook®

transforming lives together

TEN
Published by David C. Cook
4050 Lee Vance View
Colorado Springs, CO 80918 U.S.A.

David C. Cook Distribution Canada
55 Woodslee Avenue, Paris, Ontario, Canada N3L 3E5

David C. Cook U.K., Kingsway Communications
Eastbourne, East Sussex BN23 6NT, England

David C. Cook and the graphic circle C logo
are registered trademarks of Cook Communications Ministries.

The Web site addresses recommended throughout this book are offered as a
resource to you. These Web sites are not intended in any way to be or imply an
endorsement on the part of David C. Cook, nor do we vouch for their content.

Scripture taken from the *Holy Bible, New International Version*®. *NIV*®. © 1973, 1978,
1984 by International Bible Society. Used by permission of Zondervan. All rights
reserved. Scripture quotations marked NKJV are from the New King James Version.
Copyright © 1982 by Thomas Nelson, Inc. Used by permission. All rights reserved; ESV
are taken from *The Holy Bible, English Standard Version*. Copyright © 2000; 2001 by
Crossway Bibles, a division of Good News Publishers. Used by permission. All rights
reserved; MSG are taken from *THE MESSAGE*. Copyright © by Eugene Peterson 1993,
1994, 1995, 1996, 2000, 2001, 2002. Used by permission of NavPress Publishing
Group; NLT are taken from the *Holy Bible, New Living Translation*, copyright © 1996,
2004. Used by permission of Tyndale House Publishers, Inc., Wheaton, Illinois 60189

LCCN 2008937426
ISBN 978-1-4347-6729-5

© 2008 J.John

First edition published by Kingsway Communications in 2000
© J.John, ISBN 0-85476-874-2

The Team: Don Pape, Melanie Larson, Amy Kiechlin,
Jaci Schneider, and Susan Vannaman
Cover Design: JWH Graphic Arts, James Hall
Cover Photo: © 123rf.com

Printed in the United States of America
Second Edition 2008

1 2 3 4 5 6 7 8 9 10

092208

I dedicate this book to Tuana. A friend on the journey.

Contents

ACKNOWLEDGMENTS

You can't applaud with one hand. I am always grateful for the doors of opportunity—and for friends who oil the hinges. I would therefore like to acknowledge a number of people who have made this book possible. Especially my good friend Rev. Chris Russell, thank you for researching, reading, reflecting, and ruminating. Chris, you are a treasured friend who answers whenever I call. Thank you also to Belinda Russell, for her professional perspective, input, and advice on a number of issues.

Special thanks to my dear friend Dr. R. T. Kendall, whose series of sermons on the Ten Commandments and book, *Just Grace,* were so illuminating and helpful. I recommend R. T.'s book.

I am indebted to Chris and Alison Walley for their astute reading, reflection, and response to each chapter. Thank you for your time and effort.

To Gary Grant (Mr. Entertainer), you are a true friend and a tonic. Thank you for your example in taking the fourth commandment seriously.

I would like to acknowledge and thank my trustees who supervise the work I undertake—Terry and Juanita Baker, Peter Wright, Adrian Bignell, Mike Carson, and Alex Stewart-Clarke. Thank you for your counsel, support, and faith in God, who uses ordinary people like me. Thanks to all my colleagues at the Philo Trust who undergird all the work I undertake, and special thanks to my assistant, Bernadette Ocampo, who faithfully and conscientiously works as my armor bearer.

The diamonds in my life are my three sons, Michael, Simeon, and

Benjamin—they challenge me not to be theoretical about the Ten Commandments but to put them into practice! I feel privileged to have three sons entrusted to me by God, to be their soul support.

And to my partner and best friend, Killy (my wife!), whose insights added an enormous amount to each chapter and whose warmth helps us to treasure each day.

Finally, to the true and living God—you are truly perfect, powerful, and personal. You sustain us and guide us. You have blessed me with strength and purpose. Thank you for your promises. To you, Everlasting Eternal One, I am grateful.

PREFACE

This is a book on the Ten Commandments. Barely three hundred words long in English, the Ten Commandments form the foundation of our legal system, are enshrined in the heart of our parliamentary structures, and lie at the very core of Western civilization. In words so brief that they would make only a palm-size piece of text in a newspaper, this great arch of divine law encompasses family rights, property rights, the rights of the individual, and even the rights of God. Someone once said that humans are such able creatures that they have made 32,647,389 laws and still haven't been able to improve on the Ten Commandments.

Most Christians probably would admit that the Ten Commandments are important. Yet they are almost totally unknown. A recent survey of twelve hundred people aged fifteen to thirty-five found that most of those polled could name no more than two of the Ten Commandments—and they weren't too happy about some of the others when they were told about them! In speaking widely on the Ten Commandments I have been amazed at two things: the ignorance we have of them and our interest to know more about them.

The reason for the interest is, I think, pretty clear. When you look at almost all social trends, the Western world is in deep decline. We are being confronted with a rise in crime, family breakdown, personal debt, and drug abuse. We live in a generation that has lost its fixed standards. Our society isn't just a ship that has slipped loose from its moorings; it is a ship that has lost its compass and rudder, too. For a society desperately adrift, the Ten Commandments offer us both a landmark and an anchorage.

Yet there is, I believe, another reason why people are interested in the Ten Commandments today. I believe that these ancient rules are stamped—like the embossed numerals on a watch dial—onto the conscience of every man and woman. They are part of what we are as human beings, and when we hear them, we recognize them in our innermost beings.

I believe passionately that our society needs the Ten Commandments. The idea that God has rules for the way we live may sound uncomfortable and even off-putting to us today. Yet if there is a God who has made us and if he has spoken, then it makes a lot of sense to listen to what he has to say about how we run our lives. I come across many people who believe in God but don't believe God; they believe in the Maker but do not accept the Maker's instructions. That, of course, is nonsense. God himself is the source of the Ten Commandments, and because the basis of the Ten Commandments is the one who made the human race, they work.

I believe it's about time we started to take them seriously.

THE TEN COMMANDMENTS FOR THE TWENTY-FIRST CENTURY

Today there are those who would suggest that far from trying to recover the Ten Commandments for our society, it is time to modify them. They say that the Ten Commandments are obsolete. Because this is the age of democracy and personal autonomy and few of us really wish to be pushed around by commanders or commandments, these might be renamed the "Ten Suggestions." We can imagine what they might look like; instead of ten firm, nonnegotiable "Thou shalt nots," there will be only one real negative: "Do not drink and drive." The rest would be gentle exhortations to punctuality, patience, tolerance, cheerfulness, doing your best, having a sense of fair play, keeping promises, caring for the environment, and always, always putting the curtain inside the bath when you take a shower.

Others think that we do not even need to bother modifying the Commandments. We should just get rid of them. Why, they protest, should we burden modern men and women with the primitive code of a nomadic tribe that lived under skin tents in a desert? Yet the answer is that even amid vast changes, some things remain unalterable. All our ancient literature, biblical or otherwise, shows that as far as ethics goes, humans have changed not the slightest in four thousand years. We have the same vices as our ancestors. And we need the same rules.

No, the Ten Commandments are not obsolete; they are absolute. They were not made for any particular period in history. They were made for human nature and therefore were commandments for all seasons, all centuries, and all cultures. They are as universal and perpetual as honor and truth. No nation can survive apart from a moral base built on them.

There is an irony here. We have gotten rid of the Ten Commandments in the name of freedom, yet the price we have paid is our own liberty. We have pushed aside these old laws in order to have personal freedom. Yet in the resulting moral vacuum we are no longer free to venture out at night, no longer happy to let our children play on the street, and no longer able to have cars and homes without equipping them with alarms and high-tech locks. In a particularly curious twist, we have come to accept a level of video surveillance of our actions in city centers that, until recently, was applied only to inmates of high-security prisons.

Law and liberty are not in opposition. In fact, law is at the heart of liberty. Laws do not restrict us; rather they free us to live in order and harmony. This is true for societies, and it is true for individuals. Saint Augustine paraphrased the Christian law as "Love God and do what you like." Many people have gone for a different motto: "Do what you like and soon after, rush to a psychoanalyst to find out why you no longer seem to like anything."

We have come to realize that nothing is quite so enslaving as total freedom.

ABOUT THIS BOOK

The Ten Commandments occur in two places in the Bible. In Exodus 20 we have an account of how they were given to Moses on Mount Sinai, and in Deuteronomy 5 we have them repeated in the introduction to the Jewish laws. They were given to the people of Israel on their way out of slavery in Egypt to the Promised Land around 1450 BC. I have not gone into the setting here or how they were given. If you want to know the background, any good Bible dictionary, encyclopedia, or study Bible will help (I have recommended some at the end of this book).

Of the Ten Commandments, numbers one to four deal with our behavior toward God. Commandments five to nine deal with our behavior toward other people, and the tenth commandment deals with our thoughts. For each commandment, I look at the issue it addresses, try to look at the heart of the problem, and then present a series of suggestions as to how we can keep it in the twenty-first century.

I have chosen to start with the tenth commandment and end with the first. I have my reasons for, as it were, going from the outside in. The first commandment seems to me to be the glowing heart of the law, like some fiery star in the center of a planetary system. I think it is easier to spiral in slowly through the outer laws before we come face-to-face with the incandescent glow of the first commandment.

Let me also say here what this book is not. It is not some cold, analytical, intellectual study on the Ten Commandments carefully drafted on a year's sabbatical in a quiet university cloister. What I have written here has been hammered out in almost countless seminars and speaking events before tens of thousands of people. I am aware that many I speak to, and many who read this, are struggling anxiously with issues of right and wrong. Some are coming to terms with the somber implications of their moral failure. This book is not a philosophical thesis on military tactics; it is a blood-stained message from the front line. Yet isn't this how it should be? The Commandments were not given to be debated; they were given to be lived.

On this basis, there are lots of technical questions I have ducked. There is, for instance, very little here on the relationship of the sixth commandment ("You shall not murder") to warfare or capital punishment. You can't put everything in. I also am concerned about the great temptation we all have to occupy our minds with intriguing abstract problems that we do not face in order to duck dealing with the real ones that we do. For those who want to pursue matters further, there are a number of books recommended at the end of this book that may help you.

There are lots of quotes in this book, and where I can I have tried to give due credit to their authors. The eighth commandment applies to words as well as things. However, in some cases they have been bouncing about in my brain (or my study) for so long that their sources have become worn away. For the unconscious use of any such material, I ask forgiveness.

Now, let's begin our journey together into the Ten Commandments.

THE TEN
COMMANDMENTS

And God spoke all these words:

"I am the LORD your God, who brought you out of Egypt, out of the land of slavery.

"You shall have no other gods before me.

"You shall not make for yourself an idol in the form of anything in heaven above or on the earth beneath or in the waters below. You shall not bow down to them or worship them; for I, the LORD your God, am a jealous God, punishing the children for the sin of the fathers to the third and fourth generation of those who hate me, but showing love to a thousand generations of those who love me and keep my commandments.

"You shall not misuse the name of the LORD your God, for the LORD will not hold anyone guiltless who misuses his name.

"Remember the Sabbath day by keeping it holy. Six days you shall labor and do all your work, but the seventh day is a Sabbath to the LORD your God. On it you shall not do any work, neither you, nor your son or daughter, nor your manservant or maidservant, nor your animals, nor the alien within your gates. For in six days the LORD made the heavens and the earth, the sea, and all that is in them, but he rested on the seventh day. Therefore the LORD blessed the Sabbath day and made it holy.

"Honor your father and your mother, so that you may live long in the land the LORD *your God is giving you.*

"You shall not murder.

"You shall not commit adultery.

"You shall not steal.

"You shall not give false testimony against your neighbor.

"You shall not covet your neighbor's house. You shall not covet your neighbor's wife, or his manservant or maidservant, his ox or donkey, or anything that belongs to your neighbor."

Exodus 20:1–17

You shall not covet your neighbor's house. You shall not covet your neighbor's wife, or his manservant or maidservant, his ox or donkey, or anything that belongs to your neighbor.

Exodus 20:17

SO WHAT'S THE PROBLEM?

Coveting may not be a word that we use a lot today. Yet the concept of wanting what is not ours is well known. In fact, the problem that the tenth commandment addresses is so familiar that it is expressed in dozens of popular sayings and quips. Consider these:

- The biggest room in the world is the room for improvement.
- The grass is always greener on the other side of the fence.
- People live in one of two tents: content and discontent.
- Our yearnings will always exceed our earnings.

Whether it is desserts, clothes, houses, salaries, talents, lifestyles, or cars, we want what other people have. Each one of us has unique desires—we like different things, have different tastes and different priorities. It would be a boring world if we liked the same things. Yet while our desires might be different, what we all have in common with each other is this: We all want what we haven't got.

Not all desire is wrong, of course. We desire all sorts of things, in all sorts of ways. Some of our deepest desires are for good things: pleasure and joy, belonging and security, comfort and safety, excitement and adventure. We want to be well respected, to be looked up to, to be significant and loved, and to have some meaning in our lives. Those are all important things and things that we need from the moment we are born to the moment we die. Without any desire we would be little more than walking vegetables.

Yet what we aren't so aware of is that, from the moment we are born, our desires are being molded by the world around us. Soon we start to believe that the fulfillment of those good desires to be loved, to be respected, to belong, is to be found by obtaining material things. We want to be content, but we think that the only way of achieving this is by acquiring things we don't already have. We have started coveting—having an illegitimate or wrongful desire for something that, for whatever reason, is not ours to have.

The result is the mess we are in. We are a nation of people who desire what we haven't got, whether it be bank balances or brains, wives or families, houses or lifestyles. We are never satisfied! We want more and more; we want to be better and richer. It is not surprising that in a desperate—but futile—attempt to satisfy the insatiable thirst that covetousness produces, our favorite pastime is shopping.

But why start here? After all, you say, desire—even a wrong desire—is hardly a heinous crime. Aren't the other commands more important? We agree that people can, and should, be prosecuted for stealing or murder. But it is not against the law to covet. What's the big deal? What's wrong with a bit of dreaming, a bit of desiring?

Covetousness might be unseen and impossible to legislate against, but its effects are seen everywhere, and they can be devastating. Many of the darker pages of human history have resulted from covetousness. Throughout history, rulers and nations have coveted the land, resources, and wealth that belonged to others. Coveting is also one of the key factors in producing the global environmental crisis. Not only are there more people on the planet than ever before, but those people want more and more.

It is true that nobody has ever been sent down for the crime of coveting. However, you don't have to look too closely to see the effect that wrong desires have on people's actions. We might not turn all our desires into actions, but all our actions are a result of our desires. For example, every act of theft starts with someone's desire to have something that he or she has no right to have. Every act of adultery begins with someone's desire for a person he or she is not married to. Once we recognize the place that desire has in our actions, we get to deal with what is underneath the surface. Starting this way, we see the reasons that make us act in the way we do.

What is more, encouraging coveting is a major national industry; we call it advertising. Americans reportedly spend more money on advertising than on all public institutions of education, and I suspect the situation in Britain is similar. Advertisements might have been created with no goal other than to inform the public; now, they clearly set out to manipulate existing desires and create new ones. A car, house, or apartment that we have been content with for years suddenly, under the onslaught of advertisements, seems old and shabby and in urgent need of replacement.

This is what the tenth command tackles. Longing, wishing, craving, yearning, desiring—call it what we will—for what we want but cannot have. That is what coveting is all about.

Let's begin below the surface of our lives, in the place where it all starts—our hearts.

The heart of the matter

So why do we want all these things? Why is it a universal truth that men and women desire what they haven't got?

We all have desires that are God-given. For example, I believe that the desires to be loved and to feel worthwhile, to belong and to feel secure, are from God and are good. However, instead of trying to find fulfillment for them by going to our Creator God, the God who made our hearts and our desires, we go elsewhere. Let me give an example. I believe that the desire to feel significant is a good, God-given desire. Its real fulfillment lies ultimately in knowing that we are loved children of a heavenly Father. But for many people, the desire to feel significant shows itself in wearing the right clothes with the right label. With that label or designer name comes significance, and we can believe (encouraged by advertising) that by wearing it, this significance—and popularity and importance with it—is transferred to us. The right label gives our self-esteem a real boost. Or at least that's the thinking behind it. In seeking to fulfill our needs, we not only face the wrong direction but also are confused over what it is we actually do need. Why is this?

One person who succinctly explained the human dilemma nearly five hundred years ago was the Christian leader Martin Luther. He said that our basic human problem is that our hearts are "curved in on themselves." His diagnosis holds today. The person we are most concerned about in the world is our self. We are all self-obsessed. The root of covetousness is selfishness.

Why do we act like this? When God made us did he deliberately construct us to be more concerned for ourselves than anyone else? Or is it some accidental design flaw with our species?

No, we can't blame God for it. At the beginning of the Bible, in Genesis 1, we're told that God made the world, and as it tells how he reviewed the world he had created, we read, "God saw that it was good … God saw that it was good … God saw that it was good …" Man and woman too were made good; designed to enjoy the world, living together contentedly under God's rule.

Unfortunately, trouble soon came. We read in Genesis 2 how God gave humankind freedom to eat from any tree in the Garden of Eden. He gave just the one restriction: "You must not eat from the tree of the knowledge of good and evil." The Bible then describes how the devil, in the form of a serpent, tempted Adam and Eve to break this restriction. He suggested to Eve that eating the fruit would give the power to be "like God." The desire to covet—to want what was not hers to have—was sown in Eve's heart. It was an attractive offer. Imagine: being like God and having all that power, all that authority. You would be able to make all the decisions in your life; you would not have to do what anyone else said; you would not have to live in the way that someone else told you. You would have total freedom.

It was too attractive an offer, and Eve and Adam took it up and disobeyed God. The result of their disobedience lives on with us today. What they did then, we continue to do. We, too, push God off the throne and plant ourselves firmly there instead. We do what we want, we make our own decisions, we live as gods of our own lives, we love ourselves more than anything, or anyone, else.

The result is the tragedy of the human species. Our hearts were made to love God and to love others as we love ourselves. However, instead we choose to love only ourselves. As a result everyone else, God and the rest of the world, has to fall into place behind us. The effects of this total distortion of our relationships are massive.

Jesus' brother James wrote to a church that was going through difficulties: "Where do wars and fights come from among you? Do they not come from your desires for pleasure that war in your members? You lust and do not have. You murder and covet and cannot obtain. You fight and war. Yet you do not have because you do not ask" (James 4:1–2 NKJV).

Over fifteen hundred years ago, a young man called Augustine, who had been brought up in a Christian home, rebelled against everything he had been brought up to believe in and did his bit of wild living. It wasn't long before he turned again to God and then was able to say, "You have made our hearts, Lord, and they are restless until they find their rest in you." We've all got restless hearts; it is the heart disease—or disease—that is universal. One of the most famous poets of the last century, T. S. Eliot said,

> The desert is not only in remote southern tropics,
> The desert is not only around the corner,
> The desert is squeezed in the tube-train next to you,
> The desert is in the heart of your brother.
> (Choruses from The Rock I)

Recognizing the desert in our hearts, we try and pour water into it. Much of what we desire is a desperate misplaced attempt to try to irrigate our internal wasteland. This is the case in two specific areas: money and fame.

Money

We earn more now than we ever have—wages and the standard of living go up and up. Yet as they rise, so do our expectations. We live at a time that seems more covetous for money than any other time in history. Today, those who set the trends in our society are earning extraordinary sums. In 2007, *Forbes* magazine identified 946 billionaires worldwide, a record number. Two-thirds of these billionaires are richer than they were last year, and their combined net worth exceeds 3.5 trillion. Warren Buffett is the richest, with his fortune at an estimated sixty-two billion. Add to that the fact that sixty percent of these billionaires made their money from scratch! With this kind of example, is it surprising that we are all wanting more and more? John D. Rockefeller, at one time the richest man in the world, had learned this grim reality. "How much money does it take for a person to be really satisfied?" he was asked. His reply said it all: "Just a little bit more."

Coveting today is made easier by easily available credit. Items that fifty years ago a family would have had to save up for now can be bought on instant credit, creating instant debts. "Buy now, pay later" is the invitation, and "fifty-two easy payments" is the slogan. I've never met an easy payment in my life! Nowadays, people can be divided into three groups: the "haves," the "have-nots," and the "have-not-paid-for-what-they-have." Everything is faster in today's society—especially getting into debt.

Money, even vast quantities of it, fails to refresh the desert of the human heart.

Fame

We do not just covet money and things. We also covet lifestyles; we want to be other people. We all have our heroes, but so many of us go further, desiring to have their kind of life. Fame offers the illusion of an answer to our deepest needs.

Surveys tell us that 70 percent of all eighteen- to twenty-four-year-olds define success in terms of wealth and career, and that nearly two-thirds of young people feel under pressure to succeed.

In our newsstands, a whole shelf of glossy magazines parade, in multipage photo spreads, the details of the lifestyles of the famous for us to goggle at. In doing this they pander to more than our curiosity. In our hearts we want to be like them, we want to be there in those photographs, we want to be receiving phone calls from other famous stars and invited to their parties and dinners. Surely fame, we tell ourselves, will answer all our deepest needs.

Yet we know, as with money, that fame's answer is an illusion. Star after star has said it. Actress Julia Roberts has said, "I don't think I realized that the cost of fame is that it's open season on every moment of your life." Many others have echoed this sentiment, when they realize that what fame has to offer doesn't quite make them as happy as they once thought.

No matter how much we get of it, fame fails to permanently refresh the desert of the human heart.

Countering covetousness

So how do we respond? Shrug our shoulders and go and do a little shopping ourselves? Let me suggest several lines of defense against covetousness.

Beware and be realistic

Never, ever underestimate the dangerous power of covetousness. The Bible is brutally honest about the effects of wrongful desire and the fact that it can run rampant in all of us. The classic case is that of David—great psalm writer, noble warrior, and excellent king who had, it might seem, everything he could want. Yet a single case of unchecked illicit desire almost destroyed his kingship and led to untold grief.

The frank account in 2 Samuel 11 tells how one day David saw a woman bathing and, even though both of them were married, he desired her. From this act of covetousness, things spiraled inexorably downward in a tragic pattern of escalating sin. Acting on his desire, David sent for the woman, Bathsheba, and slept with her. She became pregnant, and as Uriah, her husband, had been away for months at the war, this threatened David with a considerable scandal. David, desperate for a cover-up, sent for Uriah on the assumption that he would sleep with his wife and the baby could be passed off as his. However, as a man of duty and honor in a time of war, Uriah refused to go home to his wife.

David, now in a real corner, was forced to get himself out of the mess by arranging for Uriah to be killed on the battlefield so that he could marry Bathsheba and legitimize the baby. Inevitably, the result was a disaster. God judged David and Bathsheba, and the ensuing problems came to overshadow David's entire reign. David committed adultery, abused his position as lawgiver of Israel, lied, and eventually murdered because he let his covetous desires for another man's wife overtake him. Desire in the heart leads to action. Breaking the tenth commandment resulted ultimately in David breaking the sixth, seventh, and ninth commandments as well.

Not only is covetousness powerful, it is also subtle. In fact, it can enter into almost every area of life. The Bible talks a lot about coveting, not just of things and money but also of other people's gifts or responsibilities. Paul himself appears to have found coveting a particular problem (Rom. 7:7–8). Covetousness, it seems, can easily turn followers away from Jesus and his words. In one of Jesus' stories, the sower and the seed, he talks about how people do not allow God's Word to work in their lives because they let the word become choked by the "cares and riches and pleasures of this life" (Luke 8:14 NLT).

There is even a story in the Bible that tells how, in the days of the early church, a man called Simon so coveted the miraculous gifts of the Holy Spirit that the apostles had, that he tried to buy them with money (Acts 8:4–25).

Covetousness is powerful, subtle, and can attack us in all sorts of ways, so guard every area of your life.

See through the illusion

Covetousness promises contentment and fulfillment—but it is based on an illusion. Few, if any, of the things we covet bring us either. Certainly neither riches nor fame deliver what they promise.

Ironically, this is something that, deep down, we know. In the case of money, the spectacular tales of quarrels, depression, and suicides that have resulted from the big lottery wins are so widespread that some players actually dread winning.

In the case of fame, we try and overlook the fact that those who are rich and famous often bemoan having desperately sad lives.

Remember: Covetousness promises to deliver but fails. Not only that, but in fact it does the opposite. It traps. Covetousness is deceitful; it says that if you desire things, people, lifestyles, or fame, once you get them you will be satisfied. In 1851 the German philosopher Schopenhauer said that coveting "is like sea water; the more we drink the thirstier we become."

Someone has suggested shouting, "Who are you kidding?" at ads that come on the television. Certainly we should be aware of what the underlying message is, as it is also important to teach our children how the media generally seek to manipulate our desires and confuse us over what we want and what we really need.

Let's work at understanding that things are temporary; they are not real riches. In warning his followers about covetousness Jesus told a chilling story:

> A rich man had a fertile farm that produced fine crops. He said to himself, "What should I do? I don't have room for all my crops." Then he said, "I know! I'll tear down my barns and build bigger ones. Then I'll have room enough to store all my wheat and other goods. And I'll sit back and say to myself, 'My friend, you have enough stored away for years to come. Now take it easy! Eat, drink, and be merry!'" But God said to him, "You fool! You will die this very night. Then who will get everything you worked for?" Yes, a person is a fool to store up earthly wealth but not have a rich relationship with God. (Luke 12:16–21 NLT)

Jesus pointed out how the man in this story had concluded that material possessions could satisfy all his needs. Suddenly, without warning, he was called to account and it was all taken from him.

Realize that fear feeds covetousness

It is easy to take covetousness as simply the product of greed or unchained desire. Yet the roots of covetousness are deeper. Strange as it may seem at first, I believe that one of the most fertile soils for covetousness is fear.

In today's world, fear is like the air we breathe; it's everywhere.

We fear all sorts of things, some big, some small; some that are real threats and some that are not. Recent research shows that the number-one worry people have is money. Either we worry we don't have enough or we worry about keeping what we do have.

When we face the future, we look to something for hope. Things, especially money, offer apparent security. In our fear, we focus our hopes and our confidence on things, not on God. We live as if it were all up to us—as if our survival depended on our own efforts. We take our life into our own hands, and in doing that find we have taken our life out of his.

Jesus points out the absurdity of the situation:

> Therefore I tell you, do not worry about your life, what you will eat or drink; or about your body, what you will wear. Is not life more important than food, and the body more important than clothes? Look at the birds of the air; they do not sow or reap or store away in barns, and yet your heavenly Father feeds them. Are you not much more valuable than they? (Matt. 6:25–26)

Jesus encourages people, time and time again, to trust in God, because he is faithful and true. If he looks after the birds, then of course he will look after those people who trust in him. Things provide only an illusion of security, not the reality.

Do you know which commandment is most frequently given by God to his people in the Bible? Interestingly enough, it is not one of the Ten Commandments at all. Instead, it is the command "Do not fear, do not be afraid." More than 370 times God says to his people in various ways that they needn't fear. Why? Well, obviously, not because bad things don't and can't happen, but because he is the Lord, and they can trust him with their lives. As the Christian writer Dr. Tom Wright says, this is the best news in the world because it's what we most need to hear—God addressing our fears and telling us we needn't be afraid because we can trust him.

If we knew God better, I believe we would be less tempted to be afraid. And that would cut at the very root of covetousness.

CULTIVATE CONTENTMENT

What I want to do now is to offer some positive advice about an alternative to coveting: contentment.

The old saying, "The grass is always greener on the other side of the fence," isn't automatically true. The problem is that often we have been watering it. Maybe it's time we started watering our side of the fence. Let me offer you some tips for contentment.

Keep your heart in shape

The first way we find lasting contentment is by letting God, not the world, shape our desires. God wants us first to know that he desires us and that we can trust him. Then if we will let him he will get to work on shaping our desires so that what we want is what he desires for us. The extraordinary thing is that God wants to do this.

The first thing he does is straighten out the state of our hearts—something that no fitness regime or self-help program can do. What we cannot do, God can. God made a wonderful promise through the Old Testament prophet Ezekiel: "I will give you a new heart and put a new spirit in you; I will remove from you your heart of stone and give you a heart of flesh" (Ezek. 36:26).

This heart transplant is exactly what happens when we come to know Jesus. He removes from us our old hearts, curved in on themselves, self-obsessed and selfish. In their place, he gives us his own heart. It is an extraordinary exchange. He takes our messy, malfunctioning hearts and replaces them with his. If your heart feels tired and self-obsessed, might it not be evidence that you need that heart transplant? Whoever we are, wherever we are, we need to ask him to take our old hard heart from us and give us his heart instead.

Adopt an attitude of gratitude

As we have seen, coveting does not lead to contentment, only a dissatisfaction with what we already have. The philosopher Nietzsche said, "We grow weary of those things that we most desire." Yet we read repeatedly in the Bible that one of the qualities God desires his children to have is contentment. Listen to the apostle Paul, writing from prison: "I have learned the secret of being content in any and every situation, whether well fed or hungry, whether living in plenty or in want" (Phil. 4:12).

God does not want unhealthy complaining from us. Rather he seeks the opposite outlook—what we can call "an attitude of gratitude."

It is amazing to hear Paul (again from prison) saying that he can rejoice and then go on to tell his friends to "rejoice in the Lord always" (Phil. 4:4). How could he do this in such a miserable situation? One reason is because he knew that everything he had was a gift from God. One of the problems we have in the Western world is an assumption that we deserve everything, that it is owed to us and that we have a right to it. What we fail to see is that everything we have is a gift from God. We deserve nothing.

One of the basic attitudes God desires us to have is that of thanks and praise. Coveting takes our focus away from what we already have to what we do not have, and leaves us in a guaranteed permanent state of discontent. Instead of thinking longingly, "I must have this," we should have the attitude that says gratefully, "Look at what I have already."

Take a few moments right now to think about all you have. Hasn't God been good to you?

Coveting makes us long for more; in contrast, thankfulness makes us able to see how much we already have. A man had no shoes and complained until he met a man who had no feet.

Be a wise steward

God also calls us to responsibly manage what he has given us. And that is no light matter. God has entrusted humanity with the creation he has lovingly made, with each other, and with our own abilities and resources.

The things we want and set our hearts on are not ours by right. We have done nothing to deserve them. At best, we are loaned wealth for a little while. What we are loaned is God's, and we are accountable for our use and abuse of his property.

Jesus made this point in a number of uncomfortable parables. Once, explaining how his disciples must be ready for his return, Jesus told the following story about a servant to whom the master had given the responsibility of managing his household and feeding his family.

> If the master returns and finds that the servant has done a good job, there will be a reward. I tell you the truth, the master will put that servant in charge of all he owns. But what if the servant thinks, "My master won't be back for a while," and he begins beating the other servants, partying, and getting drunk? The master will return unannounced and unexpected, and he will cut the servant in pieces and banish him with the unfaithful. And a servant who knows what the master wants, but isn't prepared and doesn't carry out those instructions, will be severely punished. But someone who does not know, and then does something wrong, will be punished only lightly. When someone has been given much, much will be required in return; and when someone has been entrusted with much, even more will be required. (Luke 12:43–48 NLT)

This whole principle—that we are stewards, not owners, of what we have—has enormous implications that space does not allow me to draw out. But we in the wealthy West should think much more about it. We have a higher standard of living than almost any other people who have ever lived, and we control so much that happens across the planet. As a result, we have an enormous and daunting responsibility to be wise and responsible stewards. We have, quite literally, been given the earth.

Focus on relationships, not things

In the pursuit of riches, things, and fame that covetousness produces, people can pay the price. In the race for prosperity, people are easily crushed in the rush. Children and families in particular can be sacrificed on the altar of overtime. Friends can fall by the wayside because of our desires for possessions or power.

God desires us to have high-quality relationships, and coveting does no good to friendships. It takes away time and opportunity, it makes us competitors, not friends, and it makes us envious and jealous of each other. How are your relationships? Are any of them suffering because you covet, because you desire things that aren't yours? If someone looked at your priorities, what impression would they get about your life?

The book of Proverbs in the Old Testament sums things up well: "Better a little with the fear of the LORD than great wealth with turmoil. Better a meal of vegetables where there is love than a fattened calf with hatred" (Prov. 15:16–17).

God's call to us is to love people and use things. Covetousness inverts this disastrously so that we end up loving things and using people.

People matter. After all, they are eternal; things aren't.

Be a giver

Perhaps the best—and certainly the most drastic—antidote for coveting is to be generous with what we have. Instead of being concerned with amassing things we should be concerned about giving them away.

At the beginning of the year 2000 the three richest people in the world together had more wealth than the poorest forty-seven countries put together. A total of 342 people had more money than half the world's population put together. We might not be in that 342, but we are rich by the standards of most of the world. Instead of grasping for more, let's learn to give it away.

Jesus talked a great deal about giving. Why? Because giving is the antidote to materialism and the infallible cure for covetousness. Jesus said, "It is more blessed to give than to receive" (Acts 20:35). As the great Christian writer C. S. Lewis so succinctly said, "Biblical charity is more than merely giving away that which we can afford to do without anyway."

Let's live simply so that others can simply live and learn again the gift of giving.

Evaluate your priorities

Complacency is very dangerous. It is a wise policy to check ourselves once in a while and make sure we haven't lost the things that money can't buy. Jesus himself said, "Beware! Guard against every kind of greed. Life is not measured by how much you own" (Luke 12:15 NLT). We all need to make priorities. Remember, if you don't live by priorities, you will live by pressures.

Let me suggest some simple questions for you:

- What do you like to think about most?
- What do you like to talk about the most?

- What do you invest most of your time and energy in?
- What do you spend your money on?
- Is there anything you would find hard to give up to save your closest relationships?

Covetousness seems the least deadly of all the Ten Commandments. Of them all, it seems the most soft-centered, the one that we can most easily live with. That is why it is so perilous. It's been said that if you drop a frog into a saucepan of hot water it will leap out. But if you put a frog in a pan of cold water and increase the temperature slowly, the frog stays there until it is boiled alive. It seems that the frog cannot see a threat in the slow, but ultimately deadly, rise in temperature. Often I wonder if that's what our society is doing to us in this whole area of our desires. All around us the temperature is going up, yet we simply sit there, stunned and unprotesting, oblivious to our impending fate.

Let's take this commandment to heart and not get boiled alive.

You shall not give false testimony against your neighbor.

Exodus 20:16

SO WHAT'S THE PROBLEM?

We are surrounded by words; from the TV and radio, through phones, in books and newspapers, on e-mails, faxes, the Internet, text messages, and sometimes—but increasingly rarely—in good old-fashioned face-to-face conversation. Words are everywhere, words are vital, but all too frequently the words are not true.

In fact we now almost don't expect that words will be true. For example, it is hard to resist smiling in disbelief when we hear any of the following:

- "The check's in the mail."
- "I'll start my diet tomorrow."
- "We believe you can't buy cheaper elsewhere."
- "One size fits all."

- "Congratulations! You have already won a free cruise to
  the Bahamas!"

The loss of truth in the public world is well known, and it seems
that barely a week goes by without some major trial centering on
claims and counterclaims of lying. Former President Bill Clinton saw
his reputation shattered worldwide because he lied live on national
television, claiming he had not had improper sexual relations with
Monica Lewinsky. Jeffrey Archer, the multimillionaire author and
politician, had to drop out of the election to be mayor of London
when it became public that he had asked one of his friends to lie for
him in court. And so on.

The problem, though, is not just in the high-profile jobs. It is at
all levels, and we have a thousand terms for it. Politicians are "eco-
nomical with the truth," statistics are "massaged," signatures and
dates are "adjusted," expenses are "inflated," and our work experience is "padded."

We lie at work (about our hours, expenses, lunch breaks, and
who really broke the copier), and we lie at home ("I thought there was
more in our account"). We lie to the taxman ("necessary expenses"),
we lie to the doctor ("I do exercise regularly"), we lie to the bank ("a
temporary shortfall"), and we lie to the traffic police ("Speed limit?
Sorry, I had no idea"). Lies are now everywhere.

The ninth commandment tackles the whole issue of truth and
lies, particularly as they affect those around us. However, this commandment is more than a simple intellectual rule that truth is good
and truth is right. It says, "You shall not give false testimony against
your neighbor." In saying that, it points out that our use and abuse

of truth affects our relationships with others. Lies are not simply wrong; lies hurt people.

Surely not! we protest. Lies are mostly harmless. But are they? The little white lie we told to shift the blame off us for the faulty product shifted it onto someone else instead; in getting ourselves off the hook, we put others on it. Adjusting our work record to make us look good makes someone else look worse. Someone, somewhere foots the bill for our creativity on our expense sheet. Lies have price tags on them that someone has to pay.

THE COST OF LYING

The consequences of this almost universal atmosphere of untruth are very serious indeed. The financial costs are astonishing, with fraudulent claims cheating the social services of hundreds of millions, if not billions, of dollars a year. Insurance companies now assume that most claims involve some element of dishonesty. The response is even more costly as society spends more and more on trying to prevent fraud with investigative teams and double-checking mechanisms. And to cover the cost of both the fraud and the preventive measures, taxes stay high and insurance premiums rise.

Other costs are less easily calculated. This acid atmosphere of lies and cynicism affects all our relationships, whether they are at work or at home. Is it any coincidence that this epidemic of lying has also been a time of unprecedented breakdown of families and marriages? I think not. All our social relations are founded upon openness and trust, and where lying prevails neither can last long. Paranoia under such circumstances is not only acceptable, it is logical; the only person you can really trust is yourself. Maybe.

IS THERE ANY TRUTH ABOUT TRUTH?

If the concept of truth is sliding down the slippery slope, then it has to be said that many philosophers have helped to grease its progress. "There is no truth," say some of them; "there is only what you think of as truth." Instead of absolute truth, they propound that there are as many relative truths as there are people on the planet. In such a relativist view the only truth that there can be is something private, personal, and individual. So what is true for you may not be true for me. There are no facts—only differing opinions.

Because of this relativist thinking, the traditional concept of history is being challenged. For instance, history is now widely seen to stand on shifting sand, with each generation and culture allowed to rewrite its past to suit its own purposes. Microsoft's version of its Encarta Encyclopedia has nine editions—American, British, French, German, Italian, Spanish, Dutch, Japanese, Brazilian—and in each one of these, history is apparently written in accord with the way those countries would like to see the past. Microsoft's director of marketing was quoted as saying, "If you look at the Battle of Waterloo in the English Encarta and the French Encarta, you get two very different versions of things, like, say, who won the battle." It is significant that science, engineering, and medicine have remained entirely immune to the charms of relativism. Scientific theories are proved true on the basis of experiments, not simply because we wish them to be true. We are given medicines because they have been demonstrated to work, not because of the pious hopes of doctors. And, thankfully, engineers rely on more than wishful thinking when it comes to assembling aircraft.

THE HEART OF THE MATTER

The Bible pulls no punches about lying. God is truth, it says, but men and women naturally prefer lies, and their reaction to Jesus demonstrates it.

The God of truth

The Bible tells us about God's character, and at the very center of it is truth. God is true—there is nothing false in him. Throughout the Bible, we see the contrast between light and darkness, goodness and evil, right and wrong, love and hatred, truth and lies. The Bible teaches that God does not just possess the characteristics of light, goodness, love, and truth—God *is* light, goodness, love, and truth.

Several times the Bible speaks of God being "the God of truth." This means that God is true in all he does and is. He is true to his word, true to his character, true to his nature. This is something unfamiliar to us. We are inconsistent, and our good character may often only be skin deep. It is common to hear in a courtroom some sad statement like "I don't know what came over him. It is most unlike him," or "She acted completely out of character." In contrast, you can never look at one of God's actions and say, "That's so unlike him." He is always true to himself; he is completely, utterly, consistently, and wonderfully true. It is interesting that Jesus (in John 8:44) terms the devil the "father of lies" as if to point out the contrast with his heavenly Father.

We know that God is truth, not just because the Bible says so, but because in Jesus we have seen God. And in Jesus we see a man who—unlike any other who has ever lived before or since—never lies or misleads. He spoke about a God of life who was stronger than death, and he rose from the grave himself. This man shows us the truth of God. Now in heaven, Jesus has not changed. He is still the truth personified.

After we accept that God is truth, we now must accept that he hears and sees our words. He knows the truth of everything about our lives, the world, and us. One of the terrifying things Jesus said is that "everything that is concealed will be brought to light and made known to all" (Luke 8:17 NLT). One day, the complete truth will be made known.

People of lies

If God is a God of truth, it is unfortunately the case that we are a people of lies. We may not lie all the time about everything, but we prefer to modify the truth far more frequently than we care to admit.

There are many different ways of lying. The most blatant form is, of course, the total lie: the complete and utter fabrication. Here someone states that what did happen didn't, or alternatively what didn't did. They say "I was never there" when they were present all the time or "I saw it all" when they were miles away. Yet there are more subtle ways to lie. There can be, for instance, the "lie of silence" when we fail to mention a significant fact. So when the boss comes in wanting to know who left the office door unlocked and we know it was us, our failure to admit it is a lie.

Then there is the lie of the misleading hint. Here we don't actually state the lie; we just assemble the pieces and let someone else put it together. So as the blame for leaving the office door open threatens us, we casually mention in a meaningful tone that the new secretary has been "very preoccupied lately" and that "she left in a hurry last night." Another danger in lying comes in the way that it deceives us about who we are. The worst lie you can tell is one to yourself. It is in this area of self-deception that the heart of lying occurs. I believe that the power of the temptation to lie comes precisely because we want to protect ourselves from the truth that shows us what we really are, rather than what we think we are.

Why do we lie? One reason for this is that we "lie to deny." We use lies to cover up who we really are and what our problems genuinely are. The other day in a national newspaper I read of a man who had completely wrecked his car and injured himself in an accident. It turned out that he was six times over the legal alcohol limit. However, rather than face up to this and admit his own responsibility, he had decided to take the owner of the pub where he had been drinking to court, claiming that as he had sold him all the drink, he was responsible.

We prefer almost anything to admitting that we are guilty. In order to deny our accountability we accumulate all sorts of explanations and excuses for our shortcomings. We say they are due to our parents, our school, our genes, our hormones. Of course, we are all, to a greater or lesser extent, products of our environment and background, and some people have been through the most appalling circumstances. But think carefully before you blame what you are on others. By doing that we are portraying ourselves as the helpless victims of events and are denying that we have the freedom and the potential to rise above our backgrounds and difficulties. Here, Christians are enormously helped by our knowledge that our Father God knows and understands what we have been through and has also given us his Holy Spirit to help us overcome our past.

Where does this universal temptation to evade responsibility come from? It is fascinating to see how early on in human history such sentiments can be found. In the previous chapter, I described how the book of Genesis tells how Adam and Eve were tempted into coveting God's position and his authority. If we jump a few verses on, we can see what happened just after they had disobeyed God.

> Then the man and his wife heard the sound of the Lord God as he was walking in the garden in the cool of the day, and they hid from the Lord God among the trees of the garden. But the Lord God called to the man, "Where are you?"
>
> He answered, "I heard you in the garden, and I was afraid because I was naked; so I hid."
>
> And he said, "Who told you that you were naked? Have you eaten from the tree that I commanded you not to eat from?"
>
> The man said, "The woman you put here with me—she gave me some fruit from the tree, and I ate it."
>
> Then the Lord God said to the woman, "What is this you have done?"
>
> The woman said, "The serpent deceived me, and I ate." (Gen. 3:8–13)

This story illustrates the heart of the problem of humanity. Adam and Eve have done something wrong so they hide—trying to get away from the consequences of what they've done. When God asks the man if he has done the one thing he had been instructed not to do, instead of owning up, Adam tries to pin the blame on Eve: "the woman you put here with me." Rather than take responsibility himself for his own actions he blames her. There is even a broad hint that, because God had put the woman in the garden, he must take some of the blame. Then, as the questioning shifts to the woman, she doesn't take responsibility either but blames the serpent—it was his fault. Now in some ways neither Adam nor Eve was lying, but neither were they telling the truth. What they obviously failed to do was admit their fault and their guilt. And so there, in the very first breaking of a command given by God, it all starts—the great human characteristic of trying to duck responsibility. Blame it on someone else, something else, anything else.

If we have any doubt that our species is fatally flawed in this area of truth, then what happened to Jesus should make us think again.

The confrontation of truth and lies

I have said that if we want to know what God is like we need to study Jesus. In Jesus' life we see God. But as we read the accounts of his life in the Gospels, we see not only the truth about God, but also the truth about human beings. At Jesus' trial and crucifixion we are shown plainly that we as human beings dislike the truth and we refuse to face up to our own responsibility.

The story of the trial of Jesus shows us what we do when we get our hands on God. A hastily convened assembly of the religious authorities summoned the arrested Jesus. They wanted to get rid of him and wanted to pass a suitable sentence on him. But to do that, they needed charges of wrongdoing. It was not easy trying to pin a charge of wrongdoing on Jesus, the Son of God! The way they achieved it was the only way possible—they lied. False allegations flew across the chamber about things he had said and about the claims he had made. We read that "many false witnesses came forward" (Matt. 26:60) and that Jesus' words were misreported and twisted. When confronted with the one human being who was completely true—who was in fact the Truth—human beings told lies about him.

Shortly after this, Jesus was summoned before the Roman governor Pontius Pilate, a man who had the power of life and death over him. All four gospel writers indicate that Pilate was unnerved by Jesus, who refused to either answer his questions or plead for his life. At one point, responding to Pilate's question as to whether he was a king, Jesus said, "'For this reason I was born, and for this I came into the world, to testify to the truth. Everyone on the side of truth listens to me.' 'What is truth?' Pilate asked" (John 18:37–38).

Pilate's pathetic question echoes down through the ages to us. Jesus, the one who is, by his own admission, "the way, the truth and the life," is just in front of him, staring him in the eyes. Yet Pilate is so blinded by lies that he cannot recognize the truth when it is standing an arm's length away from him.

I often have people say to me, "If only Jesus came now, then I'd believe." Nonsense! If he came today we would do exactly what they did with him then. First we'd try to change his views, then we'd try to silence him, and finally, when that failed, we'd kill him. Jesus wasn't executed by moronic, unbalanced lunatics, but by educated,

sophisticated, and even religious people who simply wanted to preserve the system, keep the status quo, and avoid trouble. The people
who had Jesus executed were perfectly ordinary human beings.
That's the scary thing.

There is a story about a man who was in court on a charge. At the
start of the trial he pleaded not guilty but, at the end of the first day,
he asked the judge if he could change his plea to guilty. "Why didn't
you say that earlier?" came the question from the judge. "Well, if you'll
excuse me, your honor, I didn't realize I was guilty until I heard all the
evidence." This is, if you like, what Jesus' death does to us: It shows
us what we are really like—it tells us about ourselves. What it says is
simple: When we are faced with truth we want to kill it.

We also see, in the whole sorry business of Jesus' trial, our habit
of refusing to take responsibility. Pilate, of course, famously washed
his hands, as if shedding blame for a judicial murder was as easy as
a trip to the bathroom. "It's not my fault," he said, in effect. "Don't
blame me." We have said the same ever since.

Yet if at the trial and the crucifixion humanity tries to deny
responsibility, we see on God's side something else all together. On
the cross, God in Jesus takes responsibility for the bad things we
have done. The one innocent party in the history of the human
race becomes guilty so that we might be spared guilt. It is the exact
opposite of our actions. Pilate washes his hands, desperately trying
to cleanse them of his own guilt, while Jesus extends his hands to
take on the guilt of others. As the Old Testament prophet Isaiah
predicted centuries earlier, "All of us, like sheep, have strayed away.
We have left God's paths to follow our own. Yet the Lord laid on
him the sins of us all" (Isa. 53:6 NLT).

We might not want to take responsibility for our sins, but Jesus will.

FIGHTING LIES

I want to turn now to the practicalities of how we combat our tendency to lie. As with the previous commandment, I want to start with some suggestions on how to deal with the sin itself, and then I want to move on to some ways in which we can positively affirm truth.

Beware the power of the tongue

Words have more power than we give them credit for. A preacher got up into the pulpit one Sunday morning with a big sack in his hand. "In this bag," he told the congregation, "I have the most dangerous thing in the world." He put his hand into the sack and pulled out a sword. He swung it round his head, chopped the air with it, and talked about all the terrible things that you could do with swords. Then he said, "But the most dangerous thing in the world is not a sword." He put the sword down. He reached into the bag again and pulled out a pistol. He pointed it at the ceiling and talked about the awful things you could do with guns, but then he said, "Guns are not the most dangerous thing in the world," and he put the gun down. Finally, he reached inside the bag and pulled out what looked like a long bit of red, fleshy meat. He held out the repulsive object for people to see. "This, my friends," he said solemnly, "is the most dangerous thing in the world. The tongue."

Jesus' brother James seems to have the same opinion. He tells us that the tongue is "a restless evil, full of deadly poison" (James 3:8).

Elsewhere he says that the tongue is like the rudder of a ship in that, though tiny, it steers the course and sets the direction.

The fact that words are so easily spoken also means that they can spread quickly. And in spreading they become irretrievable; once spoken we cannot take them back. There is a story of a man in the Middle Ages who confessed to a monk that he had sinned because he had been spreading rumors about someone in the local community. What should he do? The monk told him to go and put a feather on every doorstep in the community. The man rushed away, fulfilled his penance as quickly as possible, and returned to the monk. To his surprise, the monk now told him to go back and pick up all the feathers. The man protested that by now they would have been blown by the wind and would be miles away. That, the monk said, was exactly what had happened with his careless and malicious words. It is not just true of rumors; it is true of all words.

When you talk, make sure that you do so well and truthfully.

Remember the price of lying

I have already talked about the general costs of lying, particularly to society. It is good to remind ourselves of the cost of lying to us as individuals.

Even at the simplest level, lying poses problems. Telling lies often gets us in more hot water than if we had told the truth.

Lies have an extraordinary habit of growing. As Martin Luther said centuries ago, "Lies are like a snowball—as they roll, the bigger they get." To cover up a little lie we tell another and then another. Of course the more lies we tell, the greater is the danger that the whole web of deceit may start to unravel.

Lies also affect the liar. They corrode our sense of who we are and what reality is. In many lives today the line between truth and fiction has dissolved.

The liar ends up unable to trust others. This acid atmosphere of lies and cynicism affects all their relationships. "If I lie," they say to themselves, "perhaps I am lied to." Liars find it hard to know what to believe about their friends, their family, or even their lovers. Is she telling the truth? Is he? Can I trust them? Is everything lies and illusions, masks and pretences?

A more serious problem is that by lying we start to destroy our ability to detect what is wrong in our own lives. The Bible teaches that the only way we can come to know God is by admitting our wrong attitudes and actions and by repenting of them. But if we have fabricated our lives, if we no longer know who we are, then we become blinded to the fact that we need to repent. Having the habit of lying about who we are is like disabling the warning signals on a car. It gives a comforting illusion that there are no problems, but it also prevents us being warned that we may need to take serious corrective action.

Shun gossip

Earl Wilson once said, "Gossip is when you hear something you like about someone you don't." Gossip is repeating private information to someone who is neither part of the problem nor part of the solution. Gossip falls under the ninth commandment because its words are always against our neighbor and are often false. In fact one of the characteristics of gossip is that whether or not it is true isn't an issue. We tell a bit of gossip because it is a juicy tale, not because it is true. This commandment speaks against a love for gossip and intrigue about others.

The book of Proverbs talks a lot about gossip: "Without wood a fire goes out; without gossip a quarrel dies down.... The words of a gossip are like choice morsels; they go down to a man's inmost parts" (Prov. 26:20, 22).

No doubt we could all name gossips, but I'm sure we would never think of ourselves as such. We are simply interested in being kept well informed about what's going on. Of course we do sometimes say things that begin with "I shouldn't say this to you, but ..." "Have you heard about ...?" or "I am really worried about him; do you know that the other day ...?"

Gossiping can be hurtful and damaging. As I mentioned in talking about the power of our words, gossip can travel as fast and as easily as feathers in a breeze. In fact, rumors and tales are worse than feathers, for unlike them they multiply in number and size as they travel.

We have various guidelines to help us here. One thing we can do is monitor what we are saying. We might ask ourselves whether what we are about to say includes anything that might be termed gossip. If it does, we should avoid it. Another guideline is to ask ourselves, when tempted to pass on some intriguing but damaging tale: "If this was written down would I be able to sign it?" If we are not willing to put our name to a story, then we shouldn't share it. This, of course, brings us back to the fact that the ninth commandment addresses our capacity to tell lies. Yet another guideline is to ask how we would feel if the person concerned could hear us talking that way about him or her.

Yet I believe we should go further. Let's also be people who stop gossip. In fact we mustn't sit quietly by as the tales flow round us, sucking up the gossip like a vacuum cleaner. Challenge the speaker: "Are you sure?" "Have you checked this out?" "Mightn't there be another, less harmful, interpretation?" We might even say bluntly, "If you don't mind, I'd rather we didn't talk about this." Even if people may be surprised or put out when we say such things, to become known as those who don't give—or receive—gossip, is to earn respect.

It may be helpful to remember two things. First, gossips are never trusted, because they break confidences. We all know that the one who brings gossip also carries it. Second, in a curious sort of justice, those who are gossips tend to be those who attract gossip about themselves.

Avoid gossiping. There are better things to talk about.

BECOME PEOPLE OF THE TRUTH

So much for the negatives about lying. But it is not enough to reject the bad—let's take hold of the good. Being known as a man or woman of the truth means more than avoiding lies or gossip; it means affirming truth.

Facing up to the truth means being responsible for our guilt and our fallibility. It means admitting the things we do wrong and the way we sometimes don't seem to be able to help ourselves. It means that we have to avoid putting the defense of ourselves above everything, including the truth. Telling the truth is costly and uncomfortable, and it goes against our deepest nature.

Yet a moment's thought will show us that this is far from easy. Does this mean that we should never have any secrets? Does this mean that if we go to someone's new house and they ask us if we like it—and we don't—we have to tell them? What about telling "white" lies? Should we tell our children about Santa Claus or the tooth fairy? Is it ever right to lie about our age?

What I want to do now is suggest some principles so we can deal with such questions in a way that pleases God.

Be open

Clearly, most of us would accept that God doesn't want us to be barefaced liars. Nevertheless, I suggest that most of us could go much further than we do in being open.

As we have seen, our inbuilt human tendency is to lean away from honesty. We always want to cover up, to blame others, to sweep things under the carpet, to have secrets. Now, of course, there are different types of secrets. Some secrets are good and valid ones: a surprise birthday party, the home telephone number of the queen, my PIN number, your medical data. There is no reason why details of such things should be circulated. Yet there are also "bad" secrets. These are things that are unhealthy or dangerous, or things that control and obsess us. Many people have things that happened in their past that continue to haunt and cripple them today. These need to be dealt with. If you feel affected by such bad secrets, whether about yourself or another person, then I advise you to go to someone you trust (a church minister, a teacher, an accredited counselor, or, where a possible crime has occurred, the police) and arrange to talk to them about these things in confidence. It may be time to unburden yourself of something you have been carrying for years. There might be things in your past that you need to face up to or be honest about.

But openness can help well before serious problems occur. One useful safeguard is making sure that we have what is called accountability. The idea here is that you find someone you get along with, preferably someone older and wiser (and the same sex), and give them permission to ask you difficult questions about your private life. You, in turn, make a pledge not to lie to them and to be open and honest with them about your weaknesses, temptations, and struggles. By being accountable, we can be forced to face up to problems well before they get serious. If we have been honest with another person, then it becomes harder to lie to ourselves.

Be an encourager

We should speak the truth, but it is important that we always do so in love.

I knew a minister whose church was going through a tough time. The church had gone through many divisions, and people were saying things behind others' backs and even to their faces. Finally, at one meeting, the minister said, "We are going to start an MEF, a Mutual Encouragement Fellowship. We are going to encourage each other rather than discourage each other. How many want to join?"

Everyone present raised their hand.

"Well then, there's only one qualification for this—you need to think before you speak."

He then went on to explain what he meant, by giving them an acrostic for the word *THINK* based on five questions:

T—is it true?

H—will it help?

I—is it inspiring?

N—is it necessary?

K—is it kind?

As we make a commitment to telling the truth, it would be good to make a similar commitment to THINK before we speak.

One thing to be wary of as we set out to encourage each other is to avoid slipping into flattery. Flattery is insincere praise; we compliment someone—often to try and get something out of him or her—but we don't really mean what we say.

Try to honestly encourage and praise what is good. The apostle Paul provided helpful advice to the church in Philippi that we would do well to heed: "And now, dear brothers and sisters, one final thing. Fix your thoughts on what is true, and honorable, and right, and pure, and lovely, and admirable. Think about things that are excellent and worthy of praise." (Phil. 4:8 nlt).

Be true to your word

Psalm 15 starts off with the question: "Who may worship in your sanctuary, Lord?" In the four verses following, it lists the eleven characteristics of the righteous who can enter God's presence, and it is interesting that four of them center on the right use of words. One of the final characteristics, though, is challenging. It is that they are those who "keep their promises even when it hurts" (Ps. 15:4 nlt).

As people of the truth we are to be people of our word. Jesus encouraged his followers to be people who keep their word whatever the cost. He said we should let our "'yes' be 'yes,' and our 'no' be 'no'" (Matt. 5:37). Broken promises break relationships, cause hurt and pain, spread mistrust, and generate an unhealthy questioning of everything else that has ever been pledged. To be true to our word means to think carefully about what is involved before we make a promise, not after. It may mean that we need to be prepared to say no now rather than break our word later.

If we have been skeptical about the tenth commandment with its prohibition of unhealthy desires, then this ninth commandment with its reference to abuses of the tongue may seem only slightly less removed from what we think of as "real sin." Yet as we journey inward through the commandments, we can see that both raise very serious issues. The ninth commandment reminds us that speaking is a serious matter. In our modern society, we treat words far too lightly. Honesty in what we say is vital for the health of our society, for our relationships, and even for us as individuals. We should bring before God what we say, so that we may be known as trustworthy men and women whose words are both honest and fair.

You shall not steal.

Exodus 20:15

SO WHAT'S THE PROBLEM?

In our journey into the Commandments we started at the tenth commandment with our thoughts and desires and then, with the ninth commandment, moved into the world of words. Now, with the eighth commandment, we are firmly in the world of actions.

Unlike coveting or lying, the act of stealing is a physical action, and it's not just burglars and car thieves. The Web site www.cheatingculture.com estimates that 79 percent of us admit to stealing or considering stealing from our employers, and CNN reported that one out of every three businesses goes out of business because of employee theft. There are different types of stealing. Some theft, like burglary and shoplifting, is blatant and obvious. Much of this, especially where it targets our cars, houses, wallets, or handbags, seems to be against us as individuals. However, some blatant theft is impersonal, directed perhaps against a council, a company, or an organization.

Many people view those who carry out such types of direct, unashamed physical theft with a savage contempt. It is easy to demand stiff sentences for the thugs who ransack our houses or schools.

Much theft, though, is quiet and unspectacular. Apparently respectable and civilized men and women carry out far more stealing than we would like to think. Tax is evaded, mortgage applications are manipulated, grant applications are faked, and phony business loans are claimed on spurious cash-flow figures.

Another common but low-key way of stealing is in dishonest trading, where things are sold for more than they are worth. Here the line between shrewd marketing and fraudulent misrepresentation is a thin one. When we have to sell a business deal, a product, or our house, are we totally honest about both its good and bad points?

Other acts of theft get ignored because we imagine that they fall below some invisible and unwritten level of what constitutes theft. To take paper from our firm, a dozen sheets a day, is somehow acceptable, but we would never dream of walking out, once a year, with a full carton of paper. That would be stealing! We make our own phone calls from the office and acquire paper clips, pens, and Post-Its. In a thousand little ways, we steal from our employers. Time may be money in business, but we ignore that when it suits us. We have phony days off work, take extended coffee breaks, and make those little detours for shopping on our business trips. "They'll never notice," we say. "They can afford it. They owe it me. It's not really theft."

There are ironies with the current epidemic of theft that should cause us to think. On the one hand we are more prosperous now than we have ever been. Our houses are full of electronics, our wardrobes are full of clothes, our roads are full of cars, and our stores are full of consumer goods. Many of us live a lifestyle (two or more cars, regular meals out, vacations) that twenty years ago would have belonged to only the very rich. In the Western world we earn more and own more than any other people at any other time and place in history. Yet we still want more.

The problem is that in order to get what we want, many of us have no problems in helping ourselves.

THE HEART OF THE MATTER

I want now to try to look at what lies behind the extraordinary plague of stealing we have come to accept.

Things, theft, and idolatry

I believe that one factor is that we have made idols of money and things. We have already seen how the Commandments are interlocked. The tenth, ninth, and eighth commandments, with their prohibitions of coveting, lying, and theft, are all linked. It is impossible to seriously want to steal something without breaking the tenth commandment, and it is practically impossible to carry out a theft without breaking the ninth commandment. As we have seen already—and will see again—the Commandments hang together and reinforce each other. In this area of stealing, I want to suggest that yet another commandment is closely involved. This is the second commandment, which prohibits idolatry. I will talk about this in detail later, but I want to introduce the theme here now. Idolatry isn't about some gold images in a temple. It is far subtler than that. Idolatry is when things, often good in themselves, are worshipped as if they were God.

Idolatry distorts values. It elevates to ultimate importance something that is not ultimately important. It can corrupt us and lead us astray and fill us with false hopes and aspirations. This of course is not exclusively a contemporary Western problem. Jesus talked bluntly about the worship of possessions. He said, "No servant can serve two masters. Either he will hate the one and love the other, or he will be devoted to the one and despise the other. You cannot serve both God and Money" (Luke 16:13). The point here is that by making money our god, we open the door to stealing.

The epidemic of stealing that afflicts us is a result of having turned to possessions and wealth for fulfillment rather than the living God.

Whose things are they anyway?

Another factor that has affected our attitude toward stealing is our flawed understanding of possessions, as discussed in the tenth commandment.

For many people, the world and everything in it is a product of chance. Any rules to do with stealing—as with any other rules for living—arise simply because we as human beings need some sort of code to live together.

The Christian view is, of course, different. The God who made the world and who gave us the Commandments is still very much alive and active in the world today. This still is his world.

In the Old Testament we see that as David is about to reach the pinnacle of his achievements as king, he proclaims that everything he has is not his anyway—it is God's:

> Yours, O Lord, is the greatness and the power
> and the glory and the majesty and the splendor,
> for everything in heaven and earth is yours.
> Yours, O Lord, is the kingdom;
> you are exalted as head over all.
> Wealth and honor come from you;
> you are the ruler of all things.
> (1 Chron. 29:11–12)

Think about this, for it goes against many views in our modern culture. What the Bible says here—and in many other places—is stunningly simple. Ultimately everything belongs to God and nothing belongs to us. We have no rights over property or wealth. It is not ours; it is God's.

I no more own my house, my car, and my bank balance than I own my library books. They have all, in different ways, been issued to me. They remain the possessions of someone else, and one day will be returned to him. The difference is that while the librarian may then merely smile and say "thank you," God will want to know what I did with all that he lent me.

The implications of this are major in two areas. First, in the Bible's view, "our possessions" are simply on temporary loan, and we are reminded that they may be recalled to their rightful owner at any time without warning.

Second, this issue of God's ownership of everything affects stealing. When we steal, we do not wrongfully appropriate something from a company or another human being; we steal from God. That ought to make us pause.

Stealing insults God's generosity

Another factor to think about in connection with stealing is that when we steal we are denying God's care and love toward us.

God has graciously given us many gifts in creation, not because we deserve them but because God delights to bless us. We deserve nothing, yet God has given us great riches. The God who has given us life has also given us everything we need on this earth and now also sustains us. God has given so much to us that if we were to count his blessings, we would be unable to finish.

So how can we live responsibly, recognizing what God has done, without breaking the eighth commandment? How can we keep our consciences clear in this area? How can we take a stand against stealing?

STANDING UP TO STEALING

I want to show you how we can avoid theft. Then I want to show how we can adopt lifestyles and attitudes that are the opposite to the theft that the eighth commandment condemns.

Be honest about theft

Be brutally honest about your actions in this area. Very few people are prepared to look at themselves in the mirror and say, "I am a thief. I have stolen." The result is a sea of words that obscure the reality of theft. Rather than admit they stole something we hear people say that they "borrowed" it, "acquired" it, or "helped themselves." However soothing the alternative words sound, all stealing is stealing.

Sometimes something subtler occurs. Theft may be justified as a form of political or social protest. Shoplifting or the misuse of computers at work can be portrayed as a noble Robin Hood-like battle between them (who have unlimited wealth that they don't deserve) and us (who do deserve wealth). Be plain to yourself and, if necessary, to others that theft is never noble and it is never right.

Also be ruthlessly honest about what are considered more "respectable" types of theft. We feel angry revulsion at the villain who steals a television from a children's ward of a hospital. Shouldn't we feel the same revulsion at the tax evader who deprives education from valuable income?

Remember the cost of theft

All breaches of God's commandments have a cost, and this one is no different. Of course, all this has to be paid for somewhere, whether in higher prices, elevated taxes, or reduced social services. There is a direct financial cost of theft to us, whether it is having to buy burglar alarms or paying higher taxes to fund more police officers.

There are particular costs to the victims. I expect many of you reading this have been burgled (as my family has been). You can probably still remember how, as you entered your house, there was a different kind of feeling about it all; how the atmosphere seemed to have changed. Then, as you realized that your fears were true, there were the feelings of panic, of helplessness, and of being violated and defiled as you thought of an unwanted stranger going through your most private things. Such theft produces a far greater reaction than would be warranted simply by the things that have been stolen. Our safety and security, our control over our own private space, have been shattered. The scars from theft can take a long time to heal.

There are the costs, too, to those who steal. By committing a theft, a person demonstrates that he or she is a slave of money. And you cannot belong to God and money. Paul, writing to a church of new Christians at Corinth, includes thieves and swindlers in those who will not be in the kingdom of God (1 Cor. 6:9–10).

That is the bad news. The good news is that, "you were justified in the name of the Lord Jesus and by the Spirit of our God" (1 Cor. 6:11), and the Holy Spirit is able to transform the worst of thieves.

Making amends

I want to talk now about how we can adopt attitudes and lifestyles of integrity that can express the very opposite of what this commandment condemns. But before I do this, I want to deal with a difficult but vital topic. As we have seen, there are many ways for us to break the eighth commandment. What I want to say here is that if you now realize you have stolen something, then I believe it is vital that you do what you can to make amends.

One of the most extraordinary encounters Jesus had was with a man called Zacchaeus, who was the chief tax collector for the occupying Romans in Jericho (see Luke 19:1–10). Small, wealthy, probably corrupt, and certainly loathed, Zacchaeus was shown love and acceptance by Jesus when he invited himself to Zacchaeus' house for a meal. There, Zacchaeus stood up and announced that he was going to give half his possessions to the poor and that he would give back to all whom he had cheated four times the amount they had lost. In doing this, Zacchaeus was showing to everyone that he had wholehearted and genuine repentance and that he was truly and utterly sorry for what he had done. He now wanted to do all he could to put things right. Time and time again when I speak on the subject of stealing, I encourage people to return stolen goods. If they can't return them to where they came from, I suggest they hand them over to a charity or a neutral party. When I ask people to do this I know that it may be hard. When I became a Christian, I realized that I should do something about some books I had stolen from a bookshop in London. With a great deal of fear, I took them back. It was difficult and embarrassing. The first assistant I talked to nearly fainted, and I was quickly taken to the manager's office where I explained that, as a result of becoming a Christian, I now felt I had to return the stolen books. The dumbfounded manager explained that he could either call the police or bill me for the books. However, he concluded, as he had never encountered anything like this, all he could do was thank me and send me on my way. My relief as I left his office can be imagined!

Where we can, it's important to make amends for thefts we have committed in the past.

Seek integrity

Now I want to move on to how we can live a life of integrity. Integrity is the state of being innocent, trustworthy, morally upright, and free from dishonesty. The Bible makes it plain that there is more to being a follower of Jesus than simply avoiding sinful actions; rather, we are repeatedly told, we are to become more like God. We are to seek to reflect his character of openness, honesty, and justice in all that we are as individuals.

Jesus is called the good shepherd (John 10:11), who watches over the sheep flock, protecting, nurturing, and leading them. This is a perfect image of what God is like. Satan, in comparison, is described as the thief, who comes only to steal and destroy the flock (John 10:10). Stealing and robbery belong to the characteristics of the evil one. It is a sobering thought that every act of theft makes us more and more like Satan and less and less like God.

Seek integrity in personal relations

As we seek to become people of integrity, let me give two examples of practical areas where we can take action.

Determine to be honest in the way you treat other people's money. Take, for example, where you have been made a loan. Have you ever borrowed money without having any intention of paying it back? Or have you conveniently had a memory lapse about some old debt? The Bible reminds us that it is the wicked who borrow and do not repay (Ps. 37:21). If you have done either, the advice I would give you here is simple: make amends. Unpaid debts and unreturned loans can sour or ruin friendships.

This integrity does not just concern money but also applies to things. I used to own every Simon and Garfunkel album, which was a point of pride with me. I say "used to" because I so wanted friends to share my pleasure in them that I would lend them out. The result was that I haven't seen them since! Can I suggest that it may be worth looking around your attic, shed, garage, CD/DVD racks, or bookshelves for things that you have borrowed and failed to return?

Such "extended loans" are simply theft by another name. And when you find them, act! If they are in the condition they were when you were given them, give them back. If they have been damaged, worn or have otherwise suffered, then offer to replace them. Your friends who loaned them will be quite glad to see them again.

Seek integrity in work

If we need to pursue integrity in personal relationships, we also need to pursue it at work, whether your work is in an office, at home raising children, at school, or at a part-time job between jobs. What we must be wary of is laziness. I'm reminded of the manager who said to someone seeking a job, "I'm sorry I can't hire you. There isn't enough work to keep you busy," to receive the response, "You'd be surprised how little it takes." As the old proverb wisely says, the devil finds work for idle hands.

Work is good and necessary and is meant to be fulfilling and beneficial. The Bible makes it plain that we are to do our work as if we were doing it for God himself (Eph. 6:7).

Integrity applies in every area of our work. So, for example, the Bible tells us that "honest scales and balances are from the Lord" (Prov. 16:11). There is to be honesty with the tools and measures we use; there are to be no attempts to short-change people or to give them less than they require. If you are in a business in which you give quotations, make them realistic and fair. Don't rip people off.

This is also true of advertisements. Imagine if the advertising world was honest! It makes me smile just to think about it. Those who do work in that field must be morally scrupulous. Advertising, for instance, that "sells" the idea that smoking is glamorous does a disservice to young people who are blinded by imagined status. In the area of expense accounts and travel allowances, we must ask whether we handle these with integrity and complete accountability. Consider this true example of a man who was a civil servant. In the light of the Bible's teaching, he decided that he needed to take a very firm line on stealing at work. He knew it was widespread; one man's house was entirely decked out with items from work.

He determined to set an example. He decided that, instead of doing his personal photocopying on the office machine, he would walk to the nearby shop and do it during his lunch hour. Instead of using the phone on his desk for private phone calls, he would either use his cell phone during breaks or wait until he got home. His expenses were always genuine and less than the full amount that he could have claimed. His actions were inevitably noticed and brought him a bit of teasing and snide remarks. Slowly, though, everyone else around him started to act in a similar way, and within a short time the department became far more efficient and motivated. This might not automatically make us friends, but it will win us respect. It will certainly speak volumes about the different priorities we base our lives on.

But, as we have been reminded earlier, theft involves more than things or money; it also involves labor. We can steal not only by what we take physically, but also by what we refuse to give. If you are an employer, remember that the Bible says of laborers, "Pay them their wages each day before sunset because they are poor and are counting on it. If you don't, they might cry out to the LORD against you, and it would be counted against you as sin" (Deut. 24:15 NLT). This subtle form of stealing does not just occur in the workplace; it can be found in families, classrooms, and even churches. Paul in the

Bible talks about this again and again. Everybody, he says, should contribute their gifts and talents with passion and presence.

What about you? Are you holding back in any area, whether at work, home, or church? If you are, you need to be honest with yourself. It is theft, and you are stealing from those around you.

Seek corporate and national integrity

Stealing, unfortunately, can also be carried out by institutions, governments, and even nations.

The Bible is clear that our integrity extends to everything we are involved in. On this basis, we should seriously consider how our actions and investments affect the wider world. It is easy for us to buy the cheapest product at the supermarket without thinking of why it is so cheap. It is equally easy to sit back and applaud the growth in our pension funds or investments without thinking about the possible costs to others. We buy shoes or clothes without thinking that very little of the price we pay may have gone to the person who made them. The same may be true of our coffee, chocolate, or a host of other things we buy. Two hundred years ago Bible-believing Christians led the way, against considerable economic pressure, to abolish slavery in the West. It is perhaps time for us, as their descendants, to push for slavery to be abolished worldwide. After all, what greater theft can there be than making someone work for an entire lifetime for a completely inadequate wage?

Sadly, it is not just companies that are offenders here. In the Western world, we have managed to load a crippling burden of debt onto many developing countries. During the past few decades, large sums of money have been lent to poor countries by richer countries to help them fund various necessary development programs. Not only are many of these debts still there, but they have continued to grow as they amass interest. The scale of this is enormous. Significantly, Christians have been heavily involved in bringing this injustice to the attention of the Western world. The Jubilee 2000 campaign has called for the canceling of all Third World debt as the most profound and appropriate Christian gesture to mark the new millennium, and some progress has been achieved toward this.

Finally, we must look at another form of international theft. This is the area of the environment. We saw earlier that we are only stewards, rather than owners, of our own personal wealth and possessions. The same principle holds true for this world, but on a much greater scale. Although we may see ourselves as lords of creation and free to do what we want with the earth, the reality is that we are responsible to God, and one day we will be asked to account for what we allowed to happen to it. The devastation of the rain forests caused by reckless logging, the torn ozone layer produced by our CFCs, the destruction caused by our senseless burning of fossil fuels can all be seen as acts of theft against God.

We mustn't steal the future from our children. On this basis alone, Christians need to be in the forefront of the battle to reduce pollution, save resources, and preserve species.

GET THE RIGHT ATTITUDES

As we come to the end of our look at this searching and wide-ranging commandment, we should ask ourselves what other measures we can take to avoid sliding into theft. Let me remind you of three helpful attitudes to try and acquire. The first two are guidelines that we have already touched on in our dealings with the tenth commandment—hardly surprising when we see theft as the practical outworking of covetousness. The third, however, is new.

Hate greed

Greed leads to theft. We want so much that we don't mind how we get it. One problem is that we always seem to assume that when Jesus warns about the dangers of possessions, he is speaking to other people, not to us. Yet by global standards—and the standards of Jesus' day—we are all rich, and his words surely apply to us.

A bishop in South America, Dom Helder Camara, once said, "I used to think, when I was a child, that Christ might have been exaggerating when he warned about the dangers of wealth. Today I know better. I know how very hard it is to be rich and still keep the milk of human kindness. Money has a dangerous way of putting scales on one's eyes, a dangerous way of freezing people's hands, eyes, lips, and hearts."

In light of what we have seen, it might be worth taking time to examine whether wealth is pulling our lives off course. Ask yourself what you are investing your time and energy in. What are you longing for? Where is your treasure? For where our treasure is, Jesus said, there our heart will be.

Try to have a sensitive nose for the first hint of the odor of greed in your life, and learn to deal with it instantly.

Love giving

Every act of giving is an act of rebellion against a life dominated by possessions or wealth, and if we have made a practice of regular giving, then it is hard to be tempted to steal. If you have not acquired the habit of giving, I urge you to start. In fact, it is well worthwhile getting into this habit as young as possible. My wife, Killy, and I encouraged our children to learn to give early, and they have three tins for their pocket money labeled "Save," "Spend," and "Give." Such a threefold division of our wealth is no bad thing for adults either.

Let me encourage you to really think about your giving. To give away a tenth of your income is one simple principle that many people use to figure out what they should give. Of course our giving doesn't have to be only money; it can also be of time, hospitality, and material things. I believe that we have to give of ourselves as well. Let me suggest that you search your hearts for the area (whether of money, possessions, time, or something else) in which you are most tempted to steal, and make a point, in that specific area, of giving away to the extent that it hurts. I believe that giving is the best antidote for becoming a slave to possessions.

However much we give away, God has always given far more. If we are to be like him, then we too should be generous. That is one of the reasons why giving is so important. When we give we are, in a little way, imitating God.

Trust God

Finally, turn back to and rely again on the God who gives you all you need. There is a wonderful prayer recorded in the Old Testament book of Proverbs: "Two things I ask of you, O LORD.... Keep falsehood and lies far from me; give me neither poverty nor riches, but give me only my daily bread. Otherwise, I may have too much and disown you and say, 'Who is the LORD?' Or I may become poor and steal, and so dishonor the name of my God" (Prov. 30:7–9).

Learn to rely on God rather than on possessions, investments, and bank balances, and give God the space to be the provider and giver that he wants to be for us. I believe that we can rely on God for everything we need, and many times in my life I have known wonderful answers to prayer. If we do throw ourselves onto God, then our praying takes on a new dimension. Again and again Jesus encourages us to bring all our needs to our Father God. He knows what we need and is ready and waiting to give.

Trying to live the way God wants us to in the area of possessions is going to make us stand out as very strange to those we live and work with. It seems impossible. Yet what if we simply took to heart these commands to neither covet nor steal? Imagine if there was no stealing. Imagine how it would change our working relationships and environment, our friendships, our fears, our communities, our economic policy.

The point is that we are not called by Jesus to imagine a perfect world. One day that world will come. In the meantime, he simply asks us to use whatever responsibilities and gifts we have been entrusted with to make a difference.

So what are we waiting for?

You shall not commit adultery.

Exodus 20:14

So what's the problem?

Sex is inescapable. We are a society almost submerged by sex, flooded with talk about sex, innuendo about sex, images of sex, advice about sex, questionnaires about sex, assertions about sex, and problems with sex. Sex is used to grab our attention for anything. Advertisers use sex to sell cars, ice cream, toothpaste, deodorant, holidays, classical music, and even dog food.

The result is a stream of paradoxes and broken promises. The sexual revolution was supposed to bring us liberty and fulfillment, yet society seems to have more hang-ups than ever. We have—it is claimed—better sex education than ever (it is certainly more explicit), yet it results in single teenage mothers and millions of abortions each year. We are told that sex is recreational and purely for pleasure, yet we are also told that it gives our lives meaning and purpose.

Can it really be both? We have more sexual crimes than ever, and women seem to feel less safe on our streets than ever before. We find a high-tech pornography business that, on a worldwide basis, makes more money than the entire car industry. We know more about the mechanics of the orgasm than ever before, yet we seem to know less about how to make a relationship last beyond a few months. Is it possible that what we took to be the gateway to freedom was, in fact, the door to slavery?

The problem in our sex-saturated society is not that we think too much about sex, but that we think about it so poorly. There is a lack of public confidence in marriage, and the future looks stark. Fewer couples choose to marry, yet divorce is on the rise. Half of the couples who do marry choose to cohabitate before marriage, which statistically leads to even more divorces.

There are complex reasons behind these statistics, but Dr. Elaine Storkey's comments in her book *The Search for Intimacy* ring true: "Marriage … seems to have failed to provide the intimacy it promises because it has not been strong enough to withstand the pressures of stress, boredom, and financial difficulties. The argument has been that marriage, far from meeting the deepest needs of people, has often been responsible for some of their deepest problems." Certainly people have a lot of cynicism about marriage. There now seems almost a widespread expectation among marrying couples that sooner or later their own marriage will fall to bits. For many, marriage is now no longer forever.

Against this constant background noise of the selling of sex and the diluting of marriage, there has never been a greater need for clear thinking about sexual matters. The seventh commandment addresses exactly this subject. Its five words—"You shall not commit adultery"—may seem so simple that we feel we can move quickly on past them. Yet such is the confusion we now have as a society regarding sexual matters that this deserves serious discussion. You see, to understand what adultery is and why it is a sin, we need to understand what marriage is. But to understand marriage we need to understand sex. And to understand sex we need to understand the body. It is time to do some hard work.

The heart of the matter

Let me build up to the issue of marriage and adultery slowly.

The beauty of the body

The first thing to say is that God is not opposed to either sex or bodies. Actually, he cares about both more than we do. He made our physical bodies, and in Jesus—to coin a phrase—he wore one himself.

This is important. There seems to be a widely believed lie that says that God is only concerned with "spiritual" things: sacred thoughts, words and actions that are mysterious, untouchable, and angelic and a million miles away from the whole very physical (and sometimes rather messy) business of making love. Unfortunately, fairly early on in the history of Christianity the church became influenced by ancient Greek ideas and decided that bodies were bad and bodies having sex were even worse. The result was that if you wanted to be a serious Christian and become a priest, monk, or nun, you gave up the whole idea of marriage. It was only really five hundred years ago, with the rediscovery of the Bible during the Reformation period, that the equation "sex always equals sin" was broken. Yet such ideas still persist in popular culture. The same ideas occur in much religious music (those sexless pure angelic voices) and much church imagery (those unearthly stained-glass saints). They hardly encourage the idea that you can be holy and married. I mean, how do you make love when both of you wear halos?

The Bible, however, is refreshingly blunt about bodies. To take just one example, when Jesus talks about heaven and the future he frequently uses pictures of feasting and parties. It is all very down-to-earth and physical. This is important. We can't cordon God off, away from daily life; we can't ban him from the disorderliness of how we live, and we shouldn't restrict him to some mysterious part of our inner life called "spirituality." He wants to be involved in every area of our lives.

The nature of sex

God's concern about bodies extends to sex. I want to plant the flag firmly in the ground of sexuality from the start and claim it for God. He made our sex organs and gave us hormones, and far from being embarrassed by them he decided which bits should go where, and how. We read in the first chapter of Genesis how, before sin had entered the world, God made people, male and female, in his image and how it was good. In the second chapter of Genesis, it is revealed that woman and man were designed to be mutual companions and helpers and to relate to each other. Humans are unique as a species in that relationship, not reproduction, lies at the heart of the sexual act. It is presumably no accident that our species, alone of the higher animals, has intercourse face to face.

We are then, by God's design, sexual. Our sexuality, although twisted by our rebellion against God, is good and is one of his gifts. Jesus' first miracle was at a marriage feast (John 2:1–11), and wedding imagery is repeatedly used about heaven and the Second Coming in the Bible. In fact there is even a whole book in the Old Testament (the Song of Songs) that, contrary to awesome efforts of generations of preachers to make it "spiritual," is first and foremost a celebration of human love. God, the author of the Ten Commandments, is the foremost proponent of healthy sex. He is "pro-sex."

Because of the confusing times we live in, I feel, reluctantly, that I need here to make three clear points:

- To say that God is "pro-sex" is not the same as saying that he is in favor of all sexual activity. As we will see, there is only one approved context for sex, and that is inside the secure framework of a married male–female partnership. Just because I concentrate on marriage here does not mean I am not concerned about unmarrieds. To put it bluntly, it seems that those who sleep around before marriage are likely to do it afterwards.
- The Bible is absolutely clear that men and women alone were made as counterparts to each other in physical, sexual, and psychological ways. I am aware of the struggles of many in this area, and I genuinely sympathize, but I want you to understand that sexual relations between members of the same sex are plainly against God's pattern for humanity. Where homosexual or lesbian practices are mentioned in the Bible they are always condemned, often

in very strong language. There is no way that the biblical definition of marriage can be stretched to cover a same-sex relationship, however stable or long term.

- Although sex in marriage is good and God-given, I also want to point out that the Bible affirms singleness as being good. This is such an important point that I want to deal with it later.

Finally, although sex is good, it is also incredibly powerful, both for good and bad. Because the sexual relationship is at such a deep personal level, an enormous energy is linked with it. As such, sex can be destructive if misused. The illustration of sex as being like fire has much to commend it. In the right place and handled in the right way sex, like fire, can be good; misused sex—again like fire—can destroy us utterly.

The meaning of marriage

Some of the most profound truths of the Bible are contained in the first few chapters of Genesis. There we see the blueprint of what it is to be fully human. In Genesis 2 we are given the basis of marriage: "For this reason a man will leave his father and mother and be united to his wife, and they will become one flesh" (Gen. 2:24). From this we see that marriage corresponds to three things:

- *Leaving.* When a man and a woman leave the familiar world of their own families and marry, they start something new that is independent of their parents' lives. Marriage marks the irrevocable start of a new legal and social unit in the community.

- *Uniting.* A marriage is a merging of the couple in every area of life. Marriage shows a wholesale commitment between a man and a woman that brings together every aspect of what they are: personal, emotional, and social. There is to be no area where married people are to hold back from surrendering to each other.
- *Becoming one flesh.* In the sexual act, there is something far more than just physical contact happening. There is a total union, to the extent that the two people concerned are in a real sense no longer individuals.

Anything less than this total relationship falls short of the definition of marriage. To underline this all-embracing and permanent bond, the Bible talks about a marriage relationship being a "covenant." The word *covenant* means agreement or promise and comes with the implication of a lifelong commitment between two parties with mutual obligations. If we think of marriage in covenant terms, this helps us to see the place of sex within it. On the one hand, sex can be seen as the seal of the marriage relationship—the biological and spiritual equivalent of signing the wedding certificate. On the other hand, marriage provides the only safe place for sex. Only within the secure confines of a covenant relationship, where we are protected by security, love, and commitment, can the power of sex be unleashed. It should come as no surprise, then, that sex outside marriage is always seen in the Bible as dangerous and wrong.

In our society, where freedom has been elevated to be the rule of life, it is no wonder that such a binding covenant basis to marriage is disliked. I would want to argue that actually it is only by binding ourselves to each other with unbreakable commitments that we find freedom. Far from marriage restricting freedom, it actually brings freedom. We have the freedom to love another, without holding anything back. Only within the thick, secure, and private walls of a permanent marriage can we become psychologically and spiritually naked. To be loved unconditionally without strings attached, and to love in return, is true freedom.

Let me point out something about what I have just written that you may have overlooked. In the last few paragraphs I have said almost nothing at all about feelings or emotions and nothing whatsoever about "being in love." The fact is that the key elements of marriage (leaving, uniting, becoming one flesh) do not require the emotional state that the modern media insist is the only basis for marriage. And a feeling, even a strong one, on its own may fade. To hold a marriage together over many years, you need a better glue than emotions. God knows this. That's why he wants marriage to be broadly based and bound by promises. Ironically, within the secure framework of marriage where other things are doing the cementing, the emotion of love may thrive and persist.

Avoiding sexual immorality and adultery

If you have read the previous chapters, you will be able to guess my strategy in the pages ahead. What I want to do is first address the sin of sexual immorality in general and, more specifically, adultery, and show why it is so serious. Then I want to discuss how we can affirm and strengthen the institution of marriage. But before I can do either, I want to remind you to think and talk straight about sexual matters.

Be honest about sex

There are lies about every area of our lives. But there is no part of our existence where the lies are bigger, more widespread, or more seductive than in the area of sex. We must be honest and think hard in order to challenge today's sexual myths.

First of all, don't treat sex lightly. Never, ever say, as you see some scandal in the paper, "It can't happen to me." Our sexuality is such a powerful force that it is capable of tripping up presidents, politicians, princes, and even preachers. A man can labor for years with family and jobs, earning love, security, and respect from many. Then, in order to possess a few moments of sexual gratification, he throws it all away. A moment of pleasure, and a lifetime of guilt. It is extraordinary what wreckage and victims sex can produce.

Second, see through the lies. Don't be persuaded by the soft words. It may be termed by the media, or even your friends, as "a fling," "a romp," "a harmless bit of fun," or even "a romance." You should call it what it really is: immorality or adultery.

Third, remember that, as with other idols, sex promises what it cannot deliver. If you are a teenager, sex offers maturity and fulfillment. If you are lonely, sex offers closeness and companionship. If you are bored, sex offers excitement. If you are hurt, sex offers comfort. If you want to be intimate with someone, sex offers you intimacy. Yet outside the context of marriage, it actually delivers none of these things but instead gives only guilt, emptiness, and deeper hurts and regrets that are often only experienced years later.

Fourth, sexual temptation is not irresistible. To many people today, the sexual urge is something unstoppable. The urge for sex is something like a flu or cold virus. It's just in the air, and if you catch it, then hard luck. All you can do is give in to immorality. No, you need to tell yourself that wrong desires can be fought and can be defeated. Sometimes the battle is not easy, and sometimes the victory is gained at a high cost. But the biggest lie is that there is no point in resisting.

Fifth, be aware that there is more to adultery than the physical act of sex. In the pattern of marriage that I outlined earlier, of leaving, uniting, and becoming one flesh, a marriage is based on more than physical relations. Technically, it might not be adultery to have merely a deep, nonphysical, tender relationship with someone other than your spouse. But it is still an action that strikes at the heart of a marriage. The popular expression "cheating on your spouse" catches this sort of thing very well. Shun it, and work to make sure that it does not happen.

Remember the cost of adultery

If marriage is, as I have described it, an all-embracing covenant arrangement where both parties commit themselves to each other for life and give each other everything they are, sexually, psychologically, and socially, then the horror of adultery becomes plain.

Marriage is a whole web of links of intimate giving and sharing between a man and a woman, and with the act of adultery all these bonds are severed. Adultery smashes the deepest and most intimate levels of trust, shatters the covenant promises, and breaks down the walls of privacy and exclusivity that protect the heart of marriage. It is, in short, an abomination.

There are other costs. My friend Dr. Chris Bignell, who specializes in sexually transmitted diseases, recently summarized the situation for me. "People risk their physical (and psychological) health for adultery and immorality. Sexually transmitted infections are common and have a disproportionate effect on the health of women. They are a major cause of infertility, ectopic pregnancy, chronic pelvic pain, and cervical cancer." The best way to ensure you never catch a sexual disease is either not to have sex, or only to have it with someone who has only ever had sex with you. From the health point of view alone, it would be impossible to invent a better system than a lifelong exclusive marriage. God (surprise, surprise) knew what he was doing.

Adultery and immorality also affect others. Families break down, children are affected, sex crimes are on the rise, and date rape has become a reality for far too many young women.

We have as a society paid a very high price for turning our backs on the seventh commandment and on emphasizing the sexual act at the expense of relationships.

Adultery denies love, degrades people, destroys families, defiles marriage, and defies God.

Clean up your act

When I talked about theft in the last chapter, I asked you to make amends where you could. I want to be similarly practical here.

If you are involved in an adulterous relationship, end it now. Not tomorrow, not next week—now. Pick up the phone and do it. There is no easy way out, and, yes, someone is always going to get hurt, but the only way to end it is to end it. When Jesus talked about adultery, he said some strong things:

> If your right eye causes you to sin, gouge it out and
> throw it away. It is better for you to lose one part of

> your body than for your whole body to be thrown
> into hell. And if your right hand causes you to sin,
> cut it off and throw it away. It is better for you to
> lose one part of your body than for your whole
> body to go into hell. (Matt. 5:29–30)

What Jesus is saying here, beneath the imagery, is simple: Take drastic action and do some radical spiritual surgery.

Where there has been adultery, you and your marriage partner will probably need to see someone who is able to work through the issues of broken trust and violation that will be present. It is very delicate and painful and needs to be done with God's help in the context of repentance and forgiveness. But healing of a marriage can happen; I know of many cases where God has enabled restoration to occur.

In this context, I want to warn you against the peril of despair. The lie is that you cannot get out or that you can't be forgiven and made clean. I believe that with a loving, caring God, the door for repentance stays open. But if we stay in a wrong relationship, then the chances are that habit will make it harder and harder to deal with. However painful it may be, now is the time to act.

As an encouragement to you, look at one of the most powerful stories in the Gospels, where Jesus was directly confronted with adultery. In John 8:1–11 we read how the religious leaders dragged before him a woman caught in the act of adultery. In fact the text makes it plain that their real interest was to trap Jesus. Would he endorse the religious death penalty for adultery and in so doing break the Roman rule that only they could pass a death sentence? Or would he let her off and thus go against the Jewish law? So, waiting for him to condemn himself, they asked Jesus whether she should be stoned. "What do you say?" they asked. In answer, Jesus simply bent down and began writing with his finger in the dust. Incidentally, we do not know what he wrote, but it is quite possible that it was the list of the Ten Commandments. They kept badgering him for an answer until he straightened up and said, "The sinless one among you, you throw the first stone." Then as he bent down again to write some more in the dirt, they slipped away one by one, beginning with the oldest, leaving the woman alone. Jesus stood up and spoke to her. "Woman, where are they? Does no one condemn you?"

"No one, sir."

"Neither do I," said Jesus. "Go on your way. From now on, don't sin" (author's translation).

In this I see three things. First, there is a condemnation of those who were willing to use the sexual sins of others for their own purposes. Then, as now, sexual sin brings out the worst in bystanders. We need to be very careful about our own motives when we criticize in this area. Second, I see how Jesus showed mercy to the woman. He, as the one without sin, could have thrown the first stone, but he chose not to. He offers her, in effect, a new start. But third, I also see how he balances it with a requirement that she turn from her sin. I believe that he holds out the same offer of mercy matched with a call for repentance and a changed life to all who are in sexual sin today, whether in the areas of adultery, pornography, or even emotional adultery.

One of the most notorious adulterers in the Bible is King David. The Bible recounts (in 2 Sam. 12:1–14) how, under the challenging rebuke of a holy man of God, David confessed and repented of his sin. Psalm 51 was written by David at this time and is a moving model for repentance in the circumstances of sexual sin. If you have committed adultery, you would do well to spend a long time looking at and reflecting on this psalm.

I do urge you that if you are caught in this net of sin, let Jesus Christ free you. Admit to sin, confess it, repent of it, and promise to do all you can never to repeat it. Ask his power to help you overcome it.

AFFIRM MARRIAGE

Having spent some time talking about adultery and sexual sin, let me turn to how you can positively affirm marriage.

Often when I speak on this commandment I give the talk the title "How to 'Affair-Proof' Your Relationships." Adultery happens because no marriage is perfect and all of us have something in our lives—for example, a need of love, acceptance, or intimacy—that can sometimes make adultery seem attractive. I believe that God wants our marriages to be satisfying, so let me suggest what I call "The Five Rs" of a successful marriage.

Respect

Love is built on the foundation of mutual respect. Paul tells us, "Each man must love his wife as he loves himself, and the wife must respect her husband" (Eph. 5:33 NLT).

A public lecture was once advertised under the title "How to Make Your Wife Treat You Like a King." The lecture hall was absolutely packed out, with men from all sections of society waiting to hear where they were going wrong. Finally, the speaker stood up to address the packed and expectant gathering. "Gentlemen," he said to them, "the answer to the question being posed is very simple. If you want your wife to treat you like a king there is one thing you must do: treat her like a queen."

Respect is vital. The alternative is contempt, and, frankly, where there is contempt it is almost inevitable that eventually you will be in one of those dangerous conversations where you find yourself looking longingly into someone else's eyes and saying, "You know, I don't get this sort of respect at home."

Responsibility

Taking responsibility means fixing the problem, not fixing the blame. You can often see in relationships that couples spend much more time and energy attacking each other than attacking the problems. One of the things God encourages us to do is to be honest about our weaknesses and failings, to own up and take responsibility when something is our fault. Too many people stand up for their rights but fall down miserably on their responsibilities.

Not only are we to take responsibility for our own actions, but we should try to take responsibility for our partner. It is often better to pick up the blame rather than win an argument. The apostle Paul wrote to one church, "Each of you should look not only to your own interests, but also to the interests of others. Your attitude should be the same as that of Christ Jesus" (Phil. 2:4–5).

Relate

The figures on how little time couples spend together today are alarming. One Gallup poll found the average husband and wife spend less than ten minutes a day in conversation with each other. Now I know in these days we talk about quality time not quantity time, but it seems to me that nothing beats quantity quality time. Our marriages need an investment of time to nourish and cherish the relationship. We need to learn to talk and listen to each other.

Romance

I think that if there were more courting in marriage there would be fewer marriages in court! I don't know whether you were surprised by what I said earlier on in this chapter about God being pro-sex, but I am convinced not only that it is true, but that marriage is the place to demonstrate it. God, the author of the Ten Commandments, is the foremost proponent of healthy sex. Intimacy in marriage should be unashamedly erotic. As Elaine Storkey says, "A couple in marriage is called to worship God as much by their truthful, erotic sex as by their prayers for each other."

Resolve

Decide to make it work! For a successful marriage you need to make a resolve to be committed to your wife or husband not only in the one-off wedding ceremony, but also on each day of your married life. Both partners have to make a firm commitment to faithfulness, fidelity, and honesty at all times. Tell yourself that you are going to make it work or die trying.

Now please do not get me wrong. I'm not suggesting that marriages will never run into problems or have to endure storms. But I believe that the kind of commitment God is talking about means that when we hit a difficulty in our marriage, we make a decision to face it and carry on together. Trying times are not the times to stop trying. It might be that you are aware of problems in your marriage. If so, you need to be honest about those with your partner and also seek professional help. In all this, treat the gift of your marriage with the highest respect and value.

SUPPORT SINGLES

Wait a minute, you say, singles! I thought this was about marriage and adultery? It is, but I believe that the roots of many disastrous marriages go back to the mishandling of the whole issue of singleness. One reason, I believe, why there are so many disastrous marriages is that people have been so misled by our culture that they feel that they have to be married, and they are so scared of singleness that they flee from it at the earliest opportunity.

It is clear from the Bible that God calls some people to be single. I believe the single state is not for the majority, but I also believe that God equips those whom he calls that way. Singleness is not in any way an inferior or less godly way of life. It's important to find ways of integrating single people into families and communities to help meet their relational needs and affirm their value as single people. It is our job to build deep, strong, and encouraging relationships with them, so that they do not feel lonely. In particular, remember that to be called to singleness is to be called to celibacy, and as St. Augustine said, "Celibacy without community is impossible."

Although God may have called some of us to be single, he has called none of us to survive on our own. It is selfish to ignore those who are single, and we ought to do all we can to integrate singles into our lives. From my experience with singles, I have no doubt that we will benefit as much from this as they will.

GET THE RIGHT ATTITUDES

Finally, I want to suggest that we arm ourselves with the right attitudes.

Guard your minds

Whether single or married you might be thinking, "Well, I've never actually committed adultery, so how does this relate to me?" Listen to what Jesus does with this commandment in the teaching on how to live that we call the Sermon on the Mount. There he says, "You have heard that it was said, 'Do not commit adultery.' But I tell you that anyone who looks at a woman lustfully has already committed adultery with her in his heart" (Matt. 5:27–28).

What Jesus is doing is shifting the emphasis from the action back a stage further, to the desire. Clean hands are not enough; we need clean hearts. The look of lust or desire is, Jesus says, also adultery. He does not say that the look is equally as bad as the physical act, but he says that it does count as adultery. As we think about this, we realize that if our desires are to be judged, then none of us can escape condemnation. We have all sinned. This is typical of Jesus, getting at the core of the issue and reaching to examine our thoughts, our desires, and our hearts. There is a chain of things in our lives that can be summarized as follows: Thoughts become words, words become actions, actions become habits, and habits become character. We need to start at the root with thoughts.

As I close, it is worth being utterly frank about our thought life. I remember hearing of a man who had just committed adultery. "I don't know how it happened," the man protested in bewilderment to his minister. The minister turned to him and said, "I do. Had you ever committed the act in your mind with this woman?" Of course he had, and his actions had finally just followed his thoughts.

Temptation isn't wrong in itself. The question is what we do with it. The Bible encourages us to remember that "the temptations in your life are no different from what others experience. And God is faithful.… When you are tempted, he will show you a way out so that you can endure" (1 Cor. 10:13 NLT). We can't stop being bombarded by sexual images, but we can stop them getting a foothold in us. Here, though, is where we drag our wills and action into line and choose purity. The stimulus of the erotic pictures, films, and words we inevitably meet in this sex-obsessed world can play havoc with our internal desires. Many people feel enslaved and taken captive by thoughts they are ashamed of. If that describes you, then make a decision to choose God's way in this area. You don't need to live as a slave, under the domination of things that aren't pleasing to God. Allow Jesus to deliver you.

For some of you reading this, I need to issue a stronger warning. You have deliberately fed your sexual appetites. By watching particular films, reading certain magazines, visiting certain Internet sites, letting your eyes roam over whatever they choose, you have relinquished control over your own life and are heading into slavery of the most pitiable sort. If we don't confess and turn away from mental adultery and immorality, it will eventually dominate our thought life. And if we encourage it with sexually stimulating films, books, images, magazines, or social settings, our fantasy dreams will one day turn into nightmare realities.

The only solution is to deal uncompromisingly with the problem using the radical spiritual surgery that Jesus calls for. Rather than plucking out your eye, cancel the sex channel on cable television. Rather than cutting your hand off, erase those pornographic images on the computer. If you need help, then find someone wise whom you can trust to be accountable to about your internal thought life. If struggles and pain can be shared with another, they often lose their power and hold. This is nowhere more true than in this whole area of our sexuality.

Guard your behavior

It is also important that our public behavior is appropriate. In social situations, if you see someone who attracts you, for whatever reason (and we know that it happens whether we are single or married), then don't take a second look. That does not give you permission to take a long first look! In the Bible, one man of God says, "I made a covenant with my eyes not to look lustfully at a girl" (Job 31:1).

Remain aware of how your actions come across to members of the opposite sex. God wants us to have right relationships. Do you know that most affairs happen with friends? If you are married, never flirt. If you are single, never flirt unless you have a serious intent and the object of your attentions is both unattached and suitable. Keep your boundaries with members of the opposite sex clear and firm, and never give any ground for misunderstanding or ambiguity.

Choose purity today; choose God's way. I cannot encourage you enough to make up your mind to be sexually pure. Whatever you have done in the past, from this day forward you can choose purity.

A FINAL WORD

I believe that for all of us as individuals—and for our society as a whole—our sexuality is the most damaged and broken part of our humanity. Yet with God there is wholeness through healing and right relationships, through his help and his example.

In the Guinness Book of Records "Marriage" is under the category of "Human Achievement." But frankly, if we are honest here, we need more than human achievement. We need God's help. The wonderful thing though is that God does wish to help us. He, after all, is the great lover, the faithful partner, the one who is utterly committed to his covenant people. He shows he cares, not by a poem, but through cries of agony and excruciating pain. It's not champagne he drinks, but bitter wine. He doesn't bear roses in his arms, but a crown of thorns wedged on his head. He doesn't bathe us in fine-smelling perfume, but saves us through sweat and blood. God's proposal was nailed to a cross. And he did it for us. That's true love.

The only way to resist temptation to infidelity is to root our single life or our marriage in the rich soil of God's confirming love. Let go of your regrets about the past, and experience God's forgiveness and healing for previous poor choices. It is when we allow ourselves to be loved by Jesus that we are free to love like Jesus—faithfully, unconditionally, purely, and selflessly. Not for what's in it for ourselves, but for what the other person is worth.

A national newspaper ran a story a couple of years ago with the headline "Christians make the best lovers."

No wonder.

You shall not murder.

Exodus 20:13

So what's the problem?

The sixth commandment prohibits the intentional killing of a human being. As such, it seems a straightforward rule, but as we look at it, we will find ourselves forced to think about some tough matters. Most of all, and perhaps to our discomfort, we will have to look at anger, a subject that we may be all too familiar with.

For a start, though, we need to think about death. There are fashions in attitudes as well as clothes. In the Victorian age, everyone talked about death, and the taboo subject was sex. In our generation, dying and death is taboo while we are preoccupied with sex. The whole business of dying is hidden behind a screen of words: "passing away," "the departed," "chapels of rest," and so on.

Bizarrely, though, we are more familiar with death and killing than any previous generation. On our television and cinema screens, we have seen fictional death in a thousand ways. Violence is being pumped into our culture by the megaton. We have spawned a new generation of movie heroes—Rambos, Terminators, lethal weapons who Die Hard—who are not exactly walking models of "anger management." Over our popcorn, we have watched men and women shot, drowned, burned alive, crushed by cars, eaten by sharks, swallowed by snakes, consumed by aliens, and even (but more rarely) die quietly in bed.

In reality—or as near as it gets on television—we gawk at the bloodied dead of wars, shudder at the earthquake-crushed bodies, and wince at terminally malnourished infants. Then we switch channels. Occasionally, worryingly, as we stare at the screen, the worlds of reality and illusion merge. Was that film of a NATO air strike or was it a clip from a computer game? Are those really burned bodies or are they Hollywood dummies?

There are strange parallels between our modern views of sex and death. We know more about the mechanics of both sex and death than ever before, yet we seem to know less than ever about the reality and significance of either.

Our confusion is unfortunate because there is a lot of death around us. The past hundred years have seen truly horrific acts of evil against humanity: Hitler's extermination of six million Jews, the tens of millions who perished under Stalin, the millions killed in Cambodia, Uganda, and Rwanda. Famine and disease continue to kill hundreds of millions more.

The sixth commandment raises other issues. In thinking about killing and murder, matters that are literally problems of life and death emerge. How unique and valuable is a human life? How should we regard each other? How do we relate to each other? How do we cope with difference and disagreement?

The principles behind these four words, "You shall not murder," are far-reaching and go way beyond simply putting a law on the statute book.

The heart of the matter
The value of life

Life is from God. The first chapters of the Bible declare that God made heaven and earth and created men and women. Speaking of Adam, the first human, we read, "The LORD God formed the man from the dust of the ground and breathed into his nostrils the breath of life, and the man became a living being" (Gen. 2:7). Behind the pictorial language lies the plain fact that life comes from God.

Recently scientists have made all sorts of advances in the area of genetic manipulation and research; they've cloned animals and created babies in test tubes. This is still not man creating life. It is simply man copying God.

This is important. Life is not something that we automatically have or some sort of natural right. It is a gift from God. And because God alone is the one who gives life, he alone is the one who has the right to take it away. To murder is to take away someone's life. That, simply, is beyond our authority.

What is more, human life is special. We read on the first page of the Bible, "So God created human beings in his own image. In the image of God he created them; male and female he created them" (Gen. 1:27 NLT). That doesn't mean, of course, that God looks like us and has two eyes, a nose and a mouth! Rather it means that God gave us the potential, denied to all other animals, of relating to him on a personal level. It also means that we bear his image or likeness and are to show it to each other and to the world around us. We are—or were supposed to be—his representatives and little imitations of him. Additionally, the Bible reveals that God, though one being, is Father, Son, and Spirit. Between these three persons of the Trinity there is a deep relationship. As God's image bearers we show that image most when we are with other people, whether it be in a marriage, a family, or at work.

A few chapters after the story of the creation of the world we read one of God's first warnings to people: To kill a person is to kill a living being made in God's image (Gen. 9:6 NLT).

So at this point, we see there are three reasons why human life is sacred. First, God alone has the power to give life and therefore is the only one authorized to take life away.

Second, because we are made in the image of God, to take the life of another human is to destroy someone patterned after God and close to God's own heart.

Third, God made us to live together, each contributing what we have and are to others. Murder is the most brutal breach possible of that interlocked social life together.

The value of human life, all human life, is something our society today has forgotten. To treat the death of other human beings as if it were of little consequence ignores the intrinsic value of the human being. It is actually a crime against the God whose image we bear.

In the light of this, I want to look, very briefly, at some important issues of life and death that this commandment addresses. Then

I want to look at how Jesus extends the scope of this commandment so that it affects all of us.

Issues of life and death

Two groups of issues emerge here. These are whether killing in the name of the law or the state is ever right, and how we are to respond to the issues of abortion and euthanasia. Neither of them is easy, but neither of them can be ducked.

Killing under authority

I can imagine that the question has already been raised as to whether, in light of the value of the human life, it is ever right for the state to take a life. What about war or capital punishment? After all, in the time of Moses the Israelites had both. Let me briefly touch on both issues.

Killing in war

Apart from some appalling aberrations, of which the Crusades are the most notorious, almost all Christians have agreed that war is only to be undertaken as the very last, desperate resort. Every other option to resolve a situation must be tried first. There are no Christian holy wars. Some Christians have gone as far as to say that all fighting is always wrong and have taken the pacifist position. Others have said that limited and restrained wars may, at times, be justified as the lesser of a number of evils. The classic example is the defeat of Nazi Germany, which presumably spared millions from the gas chambers. The issues about justified war are complex and need more space than I have here. But we cannot escape these issues by shrugging our shoulders and hiding behind our newspapers or

Bibles. Let me give you some brief guidelines as you think this through.

- Beware of any simplistic glamorization or glorification of war, whether it is by the cinema, software makers, or the military.
- Beware of hate, the language of revenge or retaliation, or the lowering of the enemy to the subhuman level ("rats," "animals," "scum"). Wars kill men and women, mothers and children; all are made in the image of God.
- Beware of military operations expanding beyond a limited focus. When you hear terms such as "broadening the campaign," "the inflicting of unavoidable collateral damage," and "punitive air strikes," things might be going beyond any sort of justified action.

The goal for us as individuals is always clear: to pursue love, peace, and righteousness across all barriers of race, language, and culture. That—not warfare—is what will bring in God's kingdom.

Killing in punishment

Most Christians today would, I imagine, accept that capital punishment, if it is to be employed at all, is to be reserved exclusively for those who murder. There would also be, or should be, agreement that if a death sentence is carried out, it ought to be done with great sorrow and all possible dignity.

Christians who support capital punishment for murder would argue that it is precisely the value of human life that justifies the death penalty. Nothing less, they say, will show our high assessment of the victim's life. Those opposed to the death penalty would say that capital punishment is barbaric, that it dehumanizes any society that imposes it, and that, as legal systems make mistakes, we should not impose a sentence that is so irreversible. A compromise position is to propose that although the death sentence for murder should be passed (to show society's high view of life), it should always be converted to life imprisonment (to avoid the problems of enacting capital punishment). The debate will, I imagine, continue.

Killing at the beginning and end of life

Abortion. Christianity teaches that life is valuable from the moment of conception and that the child in the womb expresses consciousness, pain, and humanness. Since the legalization of abortion in the United Kingdom and the United States, millions of pregnancies have been terminated. In the United States alone, abortions have averaged more than one million per year since the 1980s.

At the outset of discussing what is a difficult and emotive topic, I want to say two things. The first is that, as a man, I feel unqualified to write about this. The responsibility for an unwanted pregnancy must be shared by a man and a woman alike, yet all too often the cost in guilt and pain is borne only by the woman. Second, I wish to try and be as sensitive as I can. I am well aware that there will be women who read this who have had abortions, often because they were pressured into them. Abortion can cause crippling guilt and regret, and I believe that God doesn't want to increase those feelings but to take them away. One book that is powerful in leading post-abortive women through the healing and forgiveness found in

Christ is *Her Choice to Heal* by Sydna Massé. You need to know and
experience the living, forgiving God who lives to heal you.

I should also say that I am not someone who believes this issue
is settled by making blanket statements and slogans. I do however
believe passionately that the current rate of abortion worldwide is
horrific and scandalous. Rape, or even alleged rape, is cited in less
than 1 percent of all abortions. Barely 1 percent of abortions occur
because there is a likelihood of fetal handicap, and only a tiny fraction of 1 percent of abortions occur because the mother's life is at
risk. In short, most abortions appear to be for convenience or as
"retroactive contraception." I think it must break God's heart to see
how this society will even dispose of its own unborn children.

In the face of such figures I believe that we must stand up for the
voiceless and question the values of a society that allow such actions
on such a scale. Having said that, I believe it is important that we offer
care, practical and financial aid, and a welcoming attitude to those
who have chosen not to terminate their pregnancy. Additionally, we
must offer education to women considering abortion and love and
understanding to those who already made the mistake. Frederica
Mathews-Green, a prolife feminist, once said, "A woman doesn't
want an abortion like she wants an ice-cream cone or a Porsche, but
like an animal caught in a trap gnaws off its own leg." These women
need wise counsel and godly friends by their sides.

Some medical students were attending a seminar on abortion
where the lecturer presented them with a case study. "The father of
the family has syphilis, and the mother, tuberculosis. They have had
four children already. The first is blind, the second died, the third is
deaf and dumb, and the fourth has tuberculosis. The mother is now

pregnant with her fifth child and is willing to have an abortion if that is what you suggest. What would your advice be?" The students overwhelmingly voted to terminate the pregnancy. "Congratulations," the lecturer responded. "You have just murdered Beethoven."

Euthanasia. The literal meaning of euthanasia is "dying well," but the term has come to mean the intentional medical termination of a person's life. It is important to distinguish euthanasia from two other practices. The first is that of allowing a patient suffering from a fatal disease to die in peace without being subjected to painful treatments that cannot ever restore him or her to health. The second is the use of pain-killing drugs to control severe pain, even at the risk of shortening life. The intention in both practices is to allow patients to end their days in as peaceful, dignified, and pain-free a way as possible. Such methods, although not without medical issues, are widely practiced and raise few significant moral problems.

In theory, euthanasia sounds harmless. The terminally ill decide voluntarily that "enough is enough" and, at the time of their choosing, are given such drugs that will cause a speedy and painless death. Supporters of euthanasia are careful to avoid any phrases that might suggest that the doctors "kill" the patient and, as with abortion, the language of "choice" and "rights" and "freedom" is widely used.

There are, however, many problems with euthanasia, particularly in providing safeguards. Proposed candidates for euthanasia are generally elderly and are almost always those who need a lot of looking after. The pressure to allow or encourage euthanasia, especially in a time of limited medical resources, can become very strong. Not even relatives can be relied on to provide a guarantee that the "right to

die" will not be abused. After all, they are probably going to benefit
from the will.

Abortion and euthanasia allow us to become judges of what is
a valid life and what isn't. The view that all human life is valuable
is not popular today, and those who object to it are plain that it is
the belief in God that is the problem. Peter Singer, the controversial
Princeton professor, bluntly expressed this fact: "Once the religious
mumbo-jumbo surrounding the term 'human' has been stripped
away … we will not regard as sacrosanct the life of every member
of our species, no matter how limited its capacity for intelligent or
even conscious life may be." In Singer's view (and he is not alone)
you have to reach some biological or mental level before you are to
be allowed to live. What those standards are, who sets them, and
whether you and I—and our children—will always reach them are
alarming and disturbing questions.

The value of all of us

Clearly the command not to murder plays a vital role in providing healthy limits to a society. Yet this commandment isn't
just about the negative concept that God is against murder. It is also
about affirming a wonderful positive truth. That truth is that we
all have value. We are to see each other as being made in the
image of God.

Now this truth relates not just to such difficult areas as war and
euthanasia, but also to everyday life. Assert, and reassert, that all
human beings are special. Let me say again that we are all made in
the image of God.

When you look at any other human being, remind yourself that in that person is reflected something of God. Because he made us in his image, we all have a priceless dignity and value.

I also want to remind you that we can break this commandment by simply doing nothing. For instance, I do not believe that we as a nation should stand passively by while genocide is committed, whether it be in Europe, Africa, or anywhere. I believe that we are in danger of committing sin by doing nothing when we ignore people in rags whom we could clothe or people who are hungry whom we could feed. If the poor freeze to death, won't we be to blame? If the hungry starve, won't we have their blood on our hands?

The roots of murder

What I have dealt with here, however briefly, are the practical issues that arise whenever we discuss murder and killing. The Bible, however, goes further and suggests that breaking the sixth commandment is not as far from each of us as we might like to think. The classic example, the prototype of this, is to be found as early in the Bible as the fourth chapter of Genesis. Here the first story of family life soon becomes the story of the first murder as Cain kills his brother Abel.

Anger and murder: episode one

I believe that the Bible tells us about Cain and Abel, not to illustrate how bad some people can get, but rather to emphasize that every one of us could end up like Cain. Cain and Abel were the sons of Adam and Eve, a family line that we all belong to. The two brothers come to bring their offerings to God. Wealthy Cain brings some of the fruit of the ground, but Abel brings the best portions of his best animals. We are told that God looked with favor on Abel's offering and not on Cain's.

What matters, it seems, is not so much the offering, but the attitude of the heart that lay behind the offering. Only Abel's motivation and attitude were acceptable to God. This annoyed Cain, and his pride was hurt. The Bible tells us what happened next: "So Cain was very angry, and his face was downcast. Then the LORD said to Cain, 'Why are you angry? Why is your face downcast? If you do what is right, will you not be accepted? But if you do not do what is right, sin is crouching at your door; it desires to have you, but you must master it'" (Gen. 4:5–7).

Notice that God here both offered Cain the possibility of change and warned him of the peril that his anger was leading him into. Yet instead of Cain looking to God in repentance, he ignored the caution, took his brother into a field, and there killed him.

Despite its antiquity, there are many ingredients in this story that we recognize. Envy, anger, deceit, lack of responsibility, lies, refusing to heed a warning, and, ultimately, murder can be found in many real-life tragedies today.

Anger and murder: Jesus makes the link

When Jesus taught on the sixth commandment he broadened the scope of it:

> You have heard that it was said to the people long ago, "Do not murder, and anyone who murders will be subject to judgment." But I tell you that anyone who is angry with his brother will be subject to judgment. Again, anyone who says to his brother,

"Raca," is answerable to the Sanhedrin. But anyone
who says, "You fool!" will be in danger of the fire of
hell. (Matt. 5:21–22)

Now I am aware that "Raca" isn't one of the top insults we hear
today. It is actually an Aramaic insult, a strong term that literally
means "empty-head" or "fool," but in a harsh, contemptuous way
that implies that the person doesn't actually deserve to be alive. The
nearest modern equivalent is probably something along the lines of
"I wish you'd never been born!" or "Do me a favor and drop dead!"

What Jesus is teaching us here is that murder is simply the ultimate
and most destructive form of anger. It is where anger, if unchecked, will
ultimately end up. God wants not only to stop the action of murder,
he wants to go further and stop those things in our thought life that
act as the seeds of murder. In the previous chapter you will remember
that Jesus did exactly the same thing with the seventh commandment.
There he pointed out that adultery was not simply the outward physical action; it was also the inward action of the heart in lust. Here he
makes it plain that the crime of murder is not simply the shedding of
blood. It is about the hatred that leads up to it.

How to handle anger

I now want to spend some time talking about how we can handle
anger.

Right anger

At the start, I need to say that not all anger is wrong. Anger is an
emotion that often shows we care. Imagine if we didn't get angry

about things; it would betray a "couldn't care less" attitude, a sort of moral apathy. St. Augustine said, "Hope has two beautiful daughters: anger and courage." Given some of the injustices in the world today, not to feel anger would be sinful.

Interestingly, the word *anger* appears 455 times in the Bible and in 375 cases it refers to God. God gets angry. Let's face it, if he didn't get angry, what kind of God would he be? God becomes angry at injustice, hypocrisy, and lies, and at people who inflict pain on each other. Jesus himself became furious in the temple at the way the changers of money and sellers of sacrifices had gotten in the way of people meeting with God.

However, there is God's righteous anger and then there is our anger. Sadly, there are differences. God is perfect and all-knowing and is always justified, both in the reason why he is angry and the way he expresses it. With us, things are both worse and more complex.

Types of human anger

When it comes to dealing with anger, at least four types of reaction can be identified.

- *The maniac.* The maniac is a pressure cooker just waiting to explode. These people have a short fuse and can blow up at any time and in any place. When they are angry, you—and everybody else around—know about it. If this is you, remember your temper is the one thing you don't get rid of by losing it!
- *The mute.* Mutes don't blow up, they clam up. They are people who cannot, or will not, show their anger in public

or in a relationship. Instead, they just bottle it up. The problem is, when we don't express our anger, our bodies keep the score. Be assured that if you try and bottle up anger it will still find other ways to come out.

- *The martyr.* Martyrs never get angry because everything is always their fault. They act like guilt magnets, always blaming themselves for what has happened. These are the people who throw a pity party and invite only themselves.

- *The manipulator.* Manipulators are those who express their anger by getting even. The situation that has annoyed them may never be mentioned again, but they make sure by their actions that they inflict revenge on the person who angered them. Some people can do this by always being late or by deliberately forgetting things.

The ancient philosopher Aristotle said, "Anyone can be angry—that is easy. But to be angry with the right person, to the right degree, at the right time, for the right purpose and in the right way—that is not easy." Let's face it, most of us do not do very well in managing our anger.

Count to ten first!

So how should we handle our anger? The book of Proverbs isolates at least three causes of anger: injustice, humiliation, and frustration. We can see here some of the things that led Cain to be angry. Causes, of course, are not excuses and do not justify anger. With Cain's anger, it seems that he felt grieved because he had expected that his offering would be accepted. It was certainly the case that he wasn't humble enough to learn a lesson and admit he had been wrong. Whenever we get angry, it is good advice to try and analyze the reasons for our anger and to be honest about them. Unfortunately, being angry is quite the wrong frame of mind in which to try to analyze anything! Attitude is the mind's paintbrush—it can color any situation.

President Lincoln's secretary of war, Edwin Stanton, had some trouble with a major general who accused him, in very abusive terms, of favoritism. Stanton complained to the president, who suggested that he write the officer a sharp letter. Stanton did so and showed the strongly worded note to the president who applauded its powerful language. "What are you going to do with it now?" he asked. Surprised at the question, Stanton said, "Send it off, of course." Lincoln shook his head. "You don't want to send that letter. Put it on the fire. That's what I do when I have written a letter while I am angry. It is a good letter, and you had a good time writing it and feel better. Now burn it and write another one."

Have self-respect and humility

We saw that one of the things that made Cain's anger burn was that he couldn't handle the fact that his younger brother was preferred over him. His previously superior position as the firstborn was overturned, and he could not cope with the reversal. His self-worth seems to have been based simply on his status.

A proper self-respect is the key to managing our anger properly. Self-respect means that we are secure enough in ourselves to know when we are in the wrong and humble enough to admit it. The problem with some people is that they think so little of themselves that they think they are always in the wrong. The problem with others is that they are so proud that they get angry because they think they are always right. We should seek a correct view of ourselves, both in humility and with self-respect. On the one hand, because God made us in his image and loves us, we are of very great worth. On the other, as weak, fallible, and sinful human beings, our assessment of ourselves may be flawed.

Deal with the anger you feel

In Matthew 5:23–24 Jesus taught that it was such a priority to deal with disagreements that if someone was worshipping and there was something between them and someone else, he or she should go and sort it out immediately. The Bible also says that we shouldn't go to sleep angry but should sort it out first.

This, of course, doesn't give us the excuse to vent; neither does it give us the right to give people a good talking to, just because they have made us unhappy. There are always two sides to each issue. Try to do everything in humility, love, and respect, and be prepared to listen to the other person's point of view. Often situations that could escalate into big fights can be prevented by our attitude. It is always very helpful to listen and refrain from making value judgments about someone else's actions or words.

Forgive—don't bear grudges

"Do not take revenge, my friends, but leave room for God's wrath, for it is written: 'It is mine to avenge; I will repay,' says the Lord" (Rom. 12:19). Our job is to forgive and not to be eaten up by our desire for revenge. It takes more inner strength to forgive than it does to inflict revenge. There are times when the most disarming thing to do in a situation of conflict is to offer appropriate apologies and forgiveness.

Forgiving others doesn't just happen because we feel like it. It happens because we make a decision of our will. Clara Barton, the founder of the American Red Cross, tried to never bear grudges. She was reminded by a friend of a wrong done to her some years earlier. "Don't you remember?" asked her friend. "No," replied Clara firmly. "I distinctly remember forgetting that."

Anger grows and festers in an atmosphere of unforgiveness and revenge. But where there is forgiveness and the decision to move on, anger can be constructive and actually good for a relationship or situation. This is how God deals with us. In the Psalms we read:

> The LORD is compassionate and merciful,
> slow to get angry and filled with unfailing love.
> He will not constantly accuse us,
> nor remain angry forever.
> He does not punish us for all our sins;
> he does not deal harshly with us, as we deserve.
> (Ps. 103:8–10 NLT)

At the start of this chapter we talked about the dignity that each one of us has because we are made in the image of God. It is in how we deal with other people that we can most reveal the fact that we bear his likeness. Are we like God in the way we deal with others? Paul encourages Christians to show the fruit of God's presence in their lives: love, joy, peace, patience, kindness, goodness, faithfulness, gentleness, and self-control (Gal. 5:22–23).

When you squeeze a tube of toothpaste, what comes out is what's in there. So it is with us. When we are squeezed, what comes out is what's inside. If we are full of God, there will be evidence of that when we are squeezed. As with the other commands we have looked at, what is necessary to be able to live God's way isn't a self-help manual but to be changed from inside out. Jesus does that by transforming us. We all need this transformation because, on Jesus' own interpretation, we have all broken the sixth commandment by our angry words and attitudes.

Find the way of love

Finally, the good news is that it is exactly with people like us that God works. Think about some of the main figures of the Bible: Moses, David, Paul. What do they all have in common? Yes, they were all followers of God, they are all credited with writing large sections of the Bible, but, astonishingly enough, they were all people who had committed murder. Yet we do not remember them for this. We remember them for what God did in and through them. And if he can do it in them, he can do it in us.

A little less than two thousand years ago God gave his Son to be murdered so that we could be given life. That death allows us to be transformed from those who hate and whose desire is to take life to those who are loving peacemakers and who want to give life. We are to be witnesses to a different way of living.

Never in the past two thousand years has that witness been more needed.

Honor your father and your mother, so that you may live long in the land the LORD your God is giving you.

Exodus 20:12

SO WHAT'S THE PROBLEM?

The endangered state of the traditional family was brought home to me recently, not by some new statistic, but by the ending of a series of television advertisements for—of all things—gravy. My non-British readers may not grasp the enormity of this, but for eighteen years, Britain had followed the Oxo family through various meal-centered stages of their life together. Finally, as the new century dawned, Oxo announced that the series had run its course because the image of Mom and Dad and three children sitting around a dining table "no longer reflected the average family." There was the need, we were told, to move with the times and portray home life in a far more varied way.

Now it is easy to be nostalgic about the "good old days" of the nuclear family with Mom, Dad, and 2.4 children. But I believe that to call for such days to be brought back is a temptation we have to resist. Memory can easily be over-romantic and selective, and behind the golden glow, painted by nostalgia, there were problems. In fact there are some current social patterns that have much to commend them: parents taking joint responsibility in the raising of children, the possibility of victims being able to get out of abusive family situations, and the empowerment and dignity that have been given to women.

But if we don't want to return to the past, neither can we be complacent about the pain and brokenness that accompany so many people's family life experiences today. Consider these figures: By the time children reach the age of sixteen, about one in four of them will have experienced the divorce of his or her parents; more than half of all marriages end in divorce; four out of ten children are now born outside marriage; and people living on their own now represent more than a quarter of all households, whereas twenty years ago the figure was 18 percent. These figures, of course, represent only the families that have failed enough to count as statistics; they do not show the far greater number of families that are under strain. Another sign of the problems is that we have absorbed a whole new vocabulary of "maintenance agreements," "access arrangements," "current partners" and "pre-nuptial agreements." And behind all these statistics and words lie real people and real lives. In fact the truth is that we don't need figures to prove any of this to us—the statistics only confirm what we have seen happen to friends, neighbors, relatives, and even ourselves.

How can the family be saved? With the pressures on the family being so great, no amount of governmental intervention, however worthy, with "Initiatives for the Family," is likely to do much good. Something more drastic is needed.

Against this background we come to the fifth commandment—to "honor your father and your mother." What, we ask, does it mean for us to honor our parents in families that are so fragmented? What can this commandment, based on a culture so different from ours, have to say to us in a world where the dysfunctional family seems to be normal?

The first thing to say is that it is easy to overestimate the differences in this area between twenty-first-century AD culture and the fifteenth-century BC Near East. Moses' day was hardly the golden age of the family either. The Bible, in its honest and unflattering way, gives us tales of families that are as spectacularly dysfunctional as any we see on our television screens. These people knew about complex and difficult families. They were just complex and difficult as ours.

The second thing to say is that in Hebrew society then, as in many similar cultures today, the key links were always up and down across the generations. That is why the Bible so often has genealogies listing how "X was the son of Y." Your bonds with your own parents, and with your children, were the cement that held families—and indeed the whole structure of society—together.

Before moving on, though, I need to spell out what it means to honor parents. Basically, it means giving them value and respect. It means esteeming them of worth, even if we disagree with them. It rules out entirely any attitude where we reject our parents as worthless.

It does not mean automatically obeying them. But I want us to avoid seeing this commandment as being exclusively to do with the relations of parents and children. It is to do with that, but it is to do with much more. Ultimately, the fifth commandment addresses the whole concept of the family.

THE HEART OF THE MATTER
The family is a gift of God

The good news is that the Bible is positive about families. The family was God's idea. If we return, as we have done before, to the earliest chapters of the Christian and Jewish Scriptures, we are struck by the fact that the family is an integral part of being human. We are meant to relate to others. God has made us and shaped us for relationships—with each other and with him. Families are the God-designed structures where we can grow and learn to understand ourselves and to relate to others. It is plain that God intended children to be raised by their natural parents and for a monogamous, lifelong male–female relationship to provide the intimate, secure, and supportive environment for a child's nurture until maturity. When, in adulthood, the child leaves his or her father and mother to start, by marriage, a new family unit, the old family links are not severed but are transformed. The new family acquires a distinct individuality of its own, but the parents are not neglected.

God affirms families. There are biblical standards for family living; norms for parental care and nurturing of children, for unconditional love, respect, and honoring of parents by offspring and a commitment to the welfare of the whole family. We may find these standards hard to keep—we may fall short of them—but they exist.

The family is always under threat

If the Bible is positive about families and sets forward the family as God's ideal, it is under no illusions that making a good family is easy. The fact that there are so many rules and guidelines about families in the Bible suggests that there have always been problems to be addressed. The stories there prove that making a family work is hard. There we see, in many of the families it records, examples of failures in this area. Some of these failures happen with even the best of men and women. For example, neither Jacob, David, nor Solomon can be held up as a model of a good father. In fact, as we saw in our discussion of murder, in the first family history recorded for us (that of Adam and Eve), relations broke down to the extent that one of their children killed another.

God intended families to be something powerful for good, to be places of belonging and trust, of learning and loving. Yet when they go wrong, their very power can make them sites of long-lasting bitterness and hurt.

But that isn't God's fault; it's ours.

God wants to help the family

Faced with these threats to the family, the encouraging news is that God does more than simply lay down a commandment and then frown at us when we mess up.

One thing God does is set us an example of how to behave in a family. He does this first of all by being the model Father who cares for and nurtures us. God endorses parenting by being happy to be considered a parent himself. This idea is there in the Old Testament and it is there, most of all, in the language of Jesus. Jesus talked of God as his Father and encouraged his disciples to use similar language. In fact the word he used, *Abba*, is respectfully intimate, and corresponds to our word *Dad*.

Some have problems with the idea of a Father God because they have had difficult relations with their own fathers. The idea that God is like such a father, only larger and in heaven, is enough to send them running. I can sympathize—I used to feel that way. It is, however, worth getting to the root of what the Bible (and Jesus) is really saying by using "father" language of God. He is not saying, "You know your dad? Well, God's like that." What he is saying is that God is everything a father should be. He is the perfect Father, the true ideal. God is like no father anyone has ever known. He is perfectly good, faithful, true, and trustworthy. He is the heavenly Father who can always be relied upon. He is the ultimate parent, like the closest, most caring guardian or the most gentle mother, and he particularly cares for those who are broken by their upbringing.

I have spent some time on this idea of God as the loving and perfect Father because it helps us to understand how we are to behave in a family context. We are to model our heavenly Father. The way he loves us is the way we should love each other, both within our families and outside them.

God does more than provide an example. He provides the power for healing in families through the Holy Spirit, whom he gives to all who have come to him through Jesus. Over and over again this comes out in the New Testament. For instance, some of the deepest teaching on families can be found in Ephesians 5:21—6:4, where Paul talks about the duties and responsibilities of wives and husbands, children and parents. But he prefaces his remarks by commanding the Ephesian Christians to let the Holy Spirit fill and control them (Eph. 5:18). The Holy Spirit is God's power for the healing of our lives with others. Only with his power can we hope to live out God's pattern for families.

CREATING FAMILIES THAT WORK

Let me now make some practical suggestions as to how we can work at making better relationships within families. I want to talk about some general principles for families, based on a biblical example; then I want to apply these to how we relate to our parents and how we relate to our children. Finally, I want to end on a note of encouragement.

Learning from failure: a biblical case study

There are good and bad ways of being family, and some patterns of living bring greater blessing than others. The best thing we can do to be part of healthy families is get into healthy patterns of behavior; not just to deal with the fallout, but to stop the hurtful behavior at the root. To illustrate some principles on which to build family life we're going to do a case study—learning from a family that lived more than three thousand years ago.

At the end of the book of Genesis is the story of Joseph, the one of Technicolor Dream Coat fame. This saga is a classic example of how families can get into bad patterns. Joseph was the son of Jacob, a man with a complex family. In the Bible the unhappy situation with Jacob's children is rapidly and skillfully painted.

> When Joseph was seventeen years old, he often tended his father's flocks. He worked for his half

> brothers, the sons of his father's wives Bilhah and
> Zilpah. But Joseph reported to his father some of
> the bad things his brothers were doing.
>
> Jacob loved Joseph more than any of his other
> children because Joseph had been born to him in
> his old age. So one day Jacob had a special gift
> made for Joseph—a beautiful robe. But his broth-
> ers hated Joseph because their father loved him
> more than the rest of them. They couldn't say a
> kind word to him. (Gen. 37:2–4 NLT)

As a result of his father's favoritism, Joseph was hated and
despised by his brothers. This is so frequently true in family life
that it is hardly surprising. Often when one child is preferred over
another it causes great consternation, jealousy, and huge feelings of
inferiority and of being overlooked. The fact that Jacob had twelve
sons by four different mothers (some wives, some concubines)
would hardly have produced a stable and secure family setting and
must have, instead, bred insecurity and competitiveness.

Matters got much worse when Joseph told his older brothers
about some dreams he'd had where the obvious interpretations
were that his brothers and his father would one day bow down to
him.

Angry, the brothers decided that enough was enough and
planned to murder Joseph and blame it on an attack by a wild animal. However, Reuben, the eldest, intervened and persuaded them
not to kill him. Finally, they agreed to a compromise and merely
threw Joseph into a pit. Reuben left, intending to come back later,

recover his brother, and take him home. But when he returned it was too late—Joseph had been sold into slavery.

Now although it would be fascinating to trace further the story of Joseph and see how, after many twists, God worked it all out for good, we cannot do it here. Yet even in this brief introduction we see a classic dysfunctional family, with its fractures developing between parents and children and between the children themselves. I think we can draw a number of general lessons from this situation about principles for family life.

Lesson 1: Learn to learn

"Learn to learn" may sound like strange advice, but it is crucial. In some ways, the most important thing we ever do is be part of a family. Yet most of us drift through, muddling along, and only really consider how we are doing when we hit a family crisis. I want to challenge you to think about how you are working in a family situation and to seek to learn how to do it better.

Jacob was a man who needed to learn. He himself had been at the rough end of some poor parenting (Gen. 26—28) involving favoritism, sibling rivalry, and a split between his parents. Yet he seems to have learned nothing from it. As we have seen, the really bad news about bad parenting is that it often gets passed on down to the next generation.

Jacob seems to have simply, dully, and automatically passed on his parents' bad habits to his children. This pattern has been repeated ever since. For example, it is said that King George V was a remote and distant man, always abrupt and cold with his children. Once, when a member of the royal court mildly suggested to the king that he might be a little more relaxed with them, he chillingly replied, "My father was frightened of his father, I was frightened of my father, and I'm damned well going to see to it that my children are frightened of me." This expresses with painful clarity the way that failure in families can, if unchecked, echo on for generations. Yet it doesn't have to be that way. Can I urge you, particularly if you are from a family that did not function well, to "learn to learn"? Try to get a chance to observe families that work, and model your behavior on them, not on your own past. Over everything you do, say to yourself, "Is this good?" or "Can I do it better?" Don't let the past ruin the future.

Lesson 2: Learn to be fair

Clearly, a major problem in the family of Jacob was his clumsy and blatant favoritism toward Joseph. Although we may not flag it quite so openly as he did, a thousand generations later favoritism is alive and well in our homes.

Avoid favoritism and unfairness in dealing with others in the family. Let's clarify what favoritism is not: an introverted, musical mother will probably have closer relations with a shy, artistic daughter than with her extrovert rugby-playing son. Favoritism is when she treats the daughter with more affection than she does the son and gives her preferential treatment. The problem of favoritism is that it hurts the child who is not favored and fuels the fires of sibling rivalry.

Incidentally, favoritism is not confined to parents with children. It is also possible for children to takes sides with one parent against another. The same principles hold true: we must be absolutely fair there, too.

Lesson 3: Learn to communicate

Another problem in Jacob's family seems to be that the family members did not communicate with each other. When I read the story, I get the feeling that here are people from the same family who do not know each other. There seems to be little evidence that the brothers ever really talked things through, either with Joseph or their father. Their hatred seems to have simmered quietly until it exploded to nearly lethal anger.

The problem has not gone away. A lot of talking in families today is simply making words, not making communication. We have all been part of a dialogue like this. A sixteen-year-old daughter went into the front room and asked the assembled family members, "Has anyone seen my new dress?"

Her dad replied, "You mean the one that cost too much?"

Her grandmother replied, "You mean the one with the low neckline?"

Her mother replied, "You mean the one that has to be washed by hand in cold water?"

Her brother replied, "The stupid one that makes you look fat?"

Her sister replied, "You mean the one that you won't let me borrow?"

Everyone was talking about the same dress, but no one answered her question. There were many words said, but no communication took place.

Good communication has to have both quantity and quality. First, good communication requires quantities of time. The most shocking statistic I heard last year was that on average a father spends thirty-eight seconds a day talking face-to-face with his children. Many young people do feel very let down by their parents simply not having the time for them. We need to make time to communicate.

Second, good communication requires quality talk. It is not enough to set aside time to talk: use it wisely. It is often good to use time to talk about life, music, films, or sports. That allows us to develop natural links. We should also be able to be honest and express irritation, hurts, and even anger. The family ought to be the best forum to discuss problems because it should be the place of security and acceptance, where people can be honest about their feelings, their expectations, and their hurts, and face them head on.

I want to make a particular plea here for fathers to become involved more in talking to their children, especially their sons. Susan Faludi, a social commentator who spent six years working on a book about masculinity published at the start of the twenty-first century, said, "From the start, I intended to talk to the young men about such matters as work, sport, marriage, religion, war, and entertainment, but what they really wanted to talk about was their fathers … 'My father never taught me how to be a man' was the single line I heard again and again."

If families don't learn to communicate with each other now, they will shout at each other later.

Lesson 4: Learn to forgive

Perhaps the most basic attitude we need is to be givers (and receivers) of grace, kindness, and forgiveness. If we are not, then not only will we carry hurts and wounds around with us, but we will pass them on to others.

The key ingredient to resolving disagreements and clashes within a family is our willingness to forgive and to be forgiven. Now of course forgiveness is never easy, and this is especially so when the other party is not sorry. Nevertheless, I believe that—for our own good, if nothing else—we must sometimes forgive unconditionally. Only that way can we release the pain we feel in being let down and hurt by members of our family and move on. Harold Bloomfield, a very respected doctor wrote in *Making Peace with Your Parents*: "The psychological truth is that holding on to our past resentments towards parents robs us of our current peace of mind and our ability to experience satisfaction in the here-and-now relationships."

To help you here I want to attack two commonly heard statements that I believe are very harmful. The first is "To forgive is to forget." I think that this belittles the horrendous experiences that some children and spouses have undergone. Many people hold back from forgiving because they incorrectly assume that if they forgive they will have to minimize (or even forget) painful things that happened to them. I can forgive my parents without minimizing the pain they caused me. Forgiveness allows us to build something positive in the present while still making sure that we don't repeat what happened in the past.

The second cliché is "Time is a great healer." It may be, but without forgiveness it is all too possible that the hurt is simply driven underground into the subconscious where it festers away. Frankly, it is important to deal with a grievance as soon as we can. Again, God helps us here. He is a God who is forgiving and gracious, and he knows all about unconditional forgiveness and what it can cost. That is what the cross was all about!

Even with the power of the Holy Spirit working in your life, I cannot, in all honesty, guarantee you a quick fix or tearless solution. But I am certain that God has all the resources you need to enable you, if you are truly willing, to forgive the one who has hurt you and to leave that resentment behind.

RELATING TO OUR PARENTS: GIVING HONOR

We've looked at qualities we are encouraged to have in our families, things that provide an environment for our children to be able to obey this command, but what does it mean to really honor our fathers and mothers? Let me here add a personal and hard-earned footnote to this advice on honoring parents. This is a hard commandment. I have struggled with what it means for me to honor my father and mother. To say that my relations with my parents have been strained is an understatement. They both refused to come to my wedding and even tried—a week before the ceremony—to bribe me into marrying another woman. It is hard to honor your parents when what they do seems to be so dishonoring to you. Yet my wife, Killy, and I have endeavored to fulfill our side of this commandment. It has not been easy.

Accept them

The first thing to do is to accept our parents. The Bible gives us some helpful advice about what that means in practice: "Listen to your father, who gave you life, and do not despise your mother when she is old" (Prov. 23:22). We are to respect our parents and not despise them.

Now, God isn't asking us to pretend that they are perfect when they are not, or that they are always right. In court, for example, we address the judge as "Your Honor." That has nothing to do with our attitude toward his or her personality; it simply shows our respect of a judge's position and authority. Likewise, "honoring" is simply an act of duty that applies to our parents.

Appreciate them

Even if we find our parents difficult, we can appreciate them for their effort in bringing us up. Parenting is a very difficult, time-consuming, and demanding job. I've said before that any mother could perform the jobs of several air-traffic controllers with ease! In fact we have probably learned far more than we think from our parents. Many of the skills, abilities, attitudes, and interests that we pride ourselves on are in fact things that have been passed on to us by our parents.

It does not hurt to find practical ways to express our appreciation. A card on Mother's Day, a regular phone call, a diversion off some trip to pass by and see Mom and Dad are all ways of appreciating them.

Affirm them

We honor our parents by affirming them. To affirm means to strengthen and support. One way we can affirm our parents is by voicing our praise to them. Praise is affirming something about someone that we know and have experienced to be true. Have you ever told your parents how grateful you are for all they gave you, for all they shaped in you, for all they taught you?

Another way to affirm our parents is by involving them in our lives. At the end of the day, we may not take their advice, for whatever reason. Yet for them, to feel that they have been consulted is a good way of honoring them.

Still another way we can affirm our parents is in the way we speak to them. Respect and regard often seem to be in very short supply when you hear the younger generation talking of those older than it. We should be more respectful in the way we talk to the older generation. After all, one day we will be part of it.

Act now

The fifth commandment has two distinctive features: It is the only one with a promise attached, and it is the only command that doesn't last a lifetime. This last point is one worth pondering. A day will come when, at a hospital bedside or in the funeral parlor, we will realize that death has removed the opportunity for us to carry out this commandment. This, then, is an urgent command.

We must not wait for a crisis, in which death threatens either us or them, to make peace with our mother and father. There are compelling reasons to start right now. To honor our parents means to obey them in our younger years, to support them in their older years, and to respect them through all the years.

RELATING TO OUR CHILDREN: EARNING HONOR

This commandment works both ways. Yes, it says that children have a duty to honor their parents. But I believe that it also implies that parents need to earn the right to be honored. Let me briefly give some suggestions as to how this might be done.

Work at parenting

Earlier, I challenged you to "learn to learn" about parenting. I repeat it now. I would, however, counsel caution about using rigid and doctrinaire methods. Parenting involves the careful use of a series of flexible skills, not the rigid, unyielding application of an exact science.

One thing that is pivotal in family life is the stability of the parental relationship. Part of the problem with Jacob's children undoubtedly came from the unstable relationships between him and the four women who bore him children. The nature and quality of the parents' relationship has lifelong consequences for the children. As we have seen elsewhere, one commandment reinforces another; keeping the "no adultery" rule is a good basis for this fifth commandment to be kept. A stable marriage is the best possible foundation for a solid family and the greatest gift any parent can give a child is to love the other parent.

I feel it is important to say something to the large number of single-parent families, whether it results from divorce, separation, or death. You belong to a group of people I especially want to affirm, and in everything I write here, I want to build you up, not pull you down. Remember that God knows you; he knows your situation, and he knows all the circumstances you face. I can only guess at how tough it is to bring up children on your own. Killy and I have found it hard enough bringing up children together. That single parents manage at all (and some manage very well) fills me with awe and respect.

Enforce discipline

Let me say something briefly here about the unpopular subject of discipline within families.

No parent enjoys discipline, and I'm sure all of us wish for families in which it is never needed. Yet the principle of discipline is

good, and indeed the Bible tells us that it is one of the characteristics
of God that he "disciplines those he loves" (Heb. 12:6). God disciplines us because he cares, because he does not want to see us hurt.
That pattern should be the model for our discipline. The purpose
of discipline is never to inflict pain or shame. It is to help teach
children, so they will learn and not harm themselves in the future. A
failure to discipline is a failure to love—a point made by the book of
Proverbs: "Those who spare the rod of discipline hate their children"
(Prov. 13:24 NLT).

The actual practice of discipline is beyond the scope of this book.
One way of imposing discipline may be the removal of privileges
(TV or computer time is a good start), but however punishment is
imposed, a number of rules must be obeyed.

- It should not be psychologically hurtful. It is worth noting
  that some nonphysical punishments, such as humiliation,
  can be very damaging.
- It should never be carried out in rage.
- It should be agreed between both parents.
- It should be appropriate to the offense.
- It should not be carried out unless there was a clear and
  willful breach of some previously defined limit.
- It should be explained.
- It should not be cruel.
- It should be followed immediately by an affirmation of love.
- Once punishment is carried out, the matter should be
  closed as the price has been paid.

And on that note let me move on to the positive counterpart to discipline: praise.

Praise them

An atmosphere of praise is the best environment for children and parents to grow in. Often parents can set an example and lead the way in this regard. One of the saddest things is to see parents who, time and time again, just grind down their children. Those children end up being crushed and without self-confidence. Yet if parents can learn to create an atmosphere of praise by being quick to compliment and credit and slow to criticize and condemn, their children will thrive and grow. Not only that, but they will be teaching them lessons on how to relate to others that will be of great blessing in the future.

Learn to let go

One couple had just had a child, but following the birth there were complications, and the baby girl had to be taken to the intensive care ward. The new mother was distraught. Later on that day, her own mother came to visit her. "Daughter," she said, "today—the day you gave birth—you have had to learn the most difficult but the most important lesson of parenting: to let them go."

Parents can nurture an atmosphere of acceptance by giving space to their children. Letting go doesn't mean letting children do anything they want, but it does mean freeing them to be themselves, letting them make their own mistakes, and letting them learn the hard way. Accepting love frees, protects, and ultimately releases.

BE ENCOURAGED

Let me end this chapter positively. Even if our experience of family has been a positive one, we would all agree that it is hard work. Both parenting and relating to parents is tough. Two mothers were talking. The first said, "My daughter doesn't tell me anything. I'm a nervous wreck." Puzzled, the second mother looked at her and replied, "My daughter tells me everything, and *I'm* a nervous wreck."

If you are struggling with parenting

If you are struggling with parenting, then let me remind you that God is for you and what you are doing. He understands. Indeed, it may help you to realize that Jesus probably understands far more than you think about running a family. You see, the last we hear of Mary's husband, Joseph, is when Jesus is twelve. Afterward there is no mention of him, and it seems probable that he died sometime before Jesus started his ministry. If this is so, then Jesus, as the eldest son, would have taken on the task of being head of a household that included a number of younger children. Yes, he does know what it is like. Not only does God sympathize, but he longs to help. He has provided us with resources in Jesus, the Holy Spirit, and the church to enable us to parent faithfully.

If you are struggling with parents

Again I'd like to remind you that God is involved in our families. In this area, too, Jesus understands. One of the most fascinating incidents in the Gospels comes when Jesus' mother, together with his brothers, came to take him away from the crowd (Mark 3:31–35). They had heard rumors of what he was doing, and we are told that they were worried he was going out of his mind, so they thought they were doing it for his sake and for the sake of the family. Jesus was forced to defend his own ministry against the well-meaning attempts of his family to intervene. Often the cry of children caught up in family difficulties is, "But no one understands." Jesus does. His family misunderstood him. If you feel everyone else is against you, make sure you remember that God knows what you are going through. Yet at the same time, Jesus was actually the model son. Some of his last words on the cross were to arrange for the apostle John to look after his mother.

Again, we see that not only does God sympathize with us, but he desires to help. Whether we are parents—or we have to deal with parents—the resources of Jesus, the Holy Spirit, and the church are available to us.

Have hope

Above all, I want you to remember that God can transform things. It is easy to be discouraged about the family. Families are an area where we all make mistakes. There are casualties of "family" everywhere—not just those openly broken families, but the ones that have tensions below the surface. Your experiences and regrets about your experience of family may have cast a mold that you feel powerless to be free from. Yet God can forgive and can change things, even the worst things.

The good news is that God wants to help us make families work. Jesus came, died, and rose again so that the gap between people and God might be healed. He also came so that the gaps between individuals might be healed.

The best and most urgently needed place for that healing is in the family.

Remember to observe the Sabbath day by keeping it holy. You have six days each week for your ordinary work, but the seventh day is a Sabbath day of rest dedicated to the LORD your God. On that day no one in your household may do any work. This includes you, your sons and daughters, your male and female servants, your livestock, and any foreigners living among you. For in six days the LORD made the heavens, the earth, the sea, and everything in them; but on the seventh day he rested. That is why the LORD blessed the Sabbath day and set it apart as holy.

Exodus 20:8–11 NLT

SO WHAT'S THE PROBLEM?

Time is relative. Albert Einstein remarked, "There certainly seems less of it about than there used to be." I wonder how often you have heard yourself say:

- "I'm too busy."
- "I don't know where all the time goes."

- "The week's simply flown."
- "I haven't had a moment to spare."

In fact, I could list many more similar sayings, but I don't have the time! Do you see the problem?

Because time is so basic and unchangeable, it is the most precious commodity we have. We are masters of so much, but, whatever our wealth, we still cannot create more time. Time passes at the same rate for the rich as it does for the poor. In fact, attempts to create more time are often counterproductive. Consider the following story:

> A business executive, talking into a cellular phone, is walking across a beautiful sun-drenched beach. Ahead of him, a man in simple clothes is dozing in the shade of a fishing boat that has been pulled up onto the beach. As the executive passes, the fisherman wakes up, and the executive, now waiting for a call to be returned, decides to make conversation.
>
> "The weather is great, there are plenty of fish; why are you lying around instead of going out and catching more?"
>
> The fisherman replies, "Because I caught enough this morning."
>
> "But just imagine," the executive says, "if you went out three or four times a day and brought home three or four times as many fish. You know what could happen?"

Puzzled, the fisherman shakes his head.

"Why," says the executive, becoming enthusiastic, "you could buy yourself a motorboat. Then after, say, two years you could buy a second one. Then after perhaps three years, you could have a cutter or two. And just think, one day you might be able to build a freezing plant—you might eventually even get your own helicopter for tracing shoals of fish and guiding your fleet of cutters. You could even acquire your own trucks to ship your fish to the capital, and then …"

"And then?" asks the fisherman.

"And then," the executive concludes triumphantly, "you could be calmly sitting at the beach side, dozing in the sun and looking at the beautiful ocean!"

The fisherman replies, "What do you think I'm doing now?"

Because time is unchanging and cannot be traded, how we use it is vital. In fact, as in so many other areas of life, when it comes to our use of time, we are in an utter mess.

Our modern lifestyles are ruthless. It is a well-known fact, proved both by statistics and experience, that although we now work harder and earn more, we have less time or energy to enjoy the money we've made. As our working hours have increased, so have our stress levels. Sixty percent of successful professionals say that they are suffering chronic stress or depression, and 48 percent of top

American corporate executives report that their lives are "empty and meaningless."

On top of earning a living, we have so much else to do today. For most of us, if we were to list everything that we had to do it would run onto several sides of paper. We have friends to phone, family members to talk to, exercise to do, appointments to make, shopping lists to write up, books to read, videos to watch, e-mails to answer, Web pages to browse, hobbies to pursue, bills to pay, and even socks to sort out! We know that our time is finite, but the demands on our time seem infinite.

Technology promised us modern conveniences that would make our lives easier, but computers, faxes, mobile phones, and e-mail have increased the pace of work rather than diminished it. Laptop computers allow us to work on the train and cell phones mean that the boss can catch us wherever we are. From transport to communications, from production to entertainment, time saved is constantly eroded, whether by greater traveling distances, more appointments, or "enhanced productivity requirements." All this ceaseless rushing around inevitably has a physical effect on us. If your body could talk, what would it say to you at this moment? I expect it would be "slow down" or "take a break." When we refuse to cooperate with God's laws for our body's proper maintenance, we run an increasing risk of malfunction. Our modern lifestyle of hustle and bustle places us in the grip of what psychologist Paul Tournier calls "universal fatigue." We constantly complain about how tired we feel. Often the first reaction we have when we wake in the morning and look at the clock is disbelief: "It can't be morning already—I'm still tired!"

In the middle of such overwhelming pressures, everyone agrees it's important to evaluate our priorities so that we can better order our lives. If we don't live by priorities, we will live by pressures.

This chapter is about the fourth commandment, where God speaks directly to us about how we order our time. One day in seven, we are told, we need to take a holy day in which we do not work. It is my strong belief, based on the Bible but supported by my own experience, that for the sake of our health, our sanity, our families, our relationships, our spirituality, and our society, we all need to have a Sabbath.

Now, let me say right at the start that we profoundly misunderstand this commandment if we think of it in any way as God making yet another burden for us. On the contrary, the Sabbath is God's gift to us. If humans were not so distorted by sin, God could perhaps have dealt with this topic in the Bible simply as a "Maker's Recommendation" along the lines of "Your Creator advises you that you will function better if you take one day in seven off." The fact is, because God knows that taking a day off is so much against our desires, he has made it a rule. In this commandment, God is ordering us to take a break.

THE HEART OF THE MATTER

You may have noticed that this is the longest of the Ten Commandments. That is not only because God wants to make it clear that it applies to everyone (sons, daughters, workers, visitors, and animals!) but also because God sets out the reasons for it being given. It is linked with how God himself works. Now, as we have seen several times already, we are made in his image, and we are patterned after him. On this basis, it is a good idea to listen carefully.

The rhythm of life

God bases his ruling of a Sabbath rest on the way that he created the universe. Now I know that there are different theories on how the first couple of chapters of the Bible are to be interpreted. I think to have an argument about whether it took God six twenty-four-hour time spans in order to make the universe sadly misses the point of what it is all about. The point of the account in Genesis is not to tell us scientifically how God created the universe; it is to tell us who made the world and why.

Into this vast universe, God himself has imprinted an order and rhythm that can be seen at every level, from how subatomic particles hold together to the way that living things interact. Whether in the cells of our body, the flow of our blood, or in the vast carbon and oxygen cycles of the atmosphere, there are regular pulses and beats as energy and elements are interchanged. The most prominent and unmistakable examples of rhythm occur in the heavens: The earth rotates on its axis, giving night and day; its path around the sun gives seasons; the moon's orbit produces monthly cycles and tides. These rhythms come from God who ordered, "Let there be lights in the expanse of the sky to separate the day from the night, and let them serve as signs to mark seasons and days and years" (Gen. 1:14).

As humans, a response to these daily, monthly, and yearly rhythms occurs at a very deep level. We sleep and wake, eat and drink, grow and develop in similar rhythmic patterns. Attempts to modify or ignore the frequency of these cycles can produce very negative results—just ask anyone with jet lag.

As if to emphasize that he is a God of rhythm, God tells us that he worked in creating the universe on a daily basis (whatever that means in terms of actual time) and that he himself rested at the end of his efforts. The principle of regular work followed by rest has therefore the highest endorsement possible: it comes from our Creator himself. Not only that, but as human beings are made in his image, this rhythm of labor followed by leisure is something that we have inherited from our heavenly Father. It's in our blood.

WHAT IS GOD'S DAY OF REST?

Before I deal with all the practical implications of what it means to keep this commandment, I need to discuss briefly what God's day of rest is.

A brief history of God's day of rest

The commandment, as it was originally given, refers to the seventh day of the week—our Saturday. Keeping the Sabbath by refraining from all work and holding religious services was one of the great distinguishing marks of the Jewish faith in the Bible—a tradition that modern Judaism has kept. In the Old Testament there are various other laws that were given about the Sabbath that strictly limited the extent to which, for example, you could travel or prepare food. In the Gospels, we see that Jesus and his disciples attended the synagogue services on the Sabbath, and presumably they kept the Sabbath rules given in the Old Testament. By Jesus' day, however, the God-given Old Testament laws on the Sabbath had been added to by a vast number of restrictive and often petty rules from the religious authorities. Jesus came into conflict with these and had a number of disputes with the religious leaders about what the purpose of the Sabbath really was. This is something that I will talk more about later.

After the resurrection of Jesus something very remarkable happened. Although most of the first Christians were Jewish and kept the old Sabbath, very soon Christians started worshipping on the Sunday, the first day of the week. The fact that the resurrection had occurred on a Sunday must have been the key factor in making the switch. That the Holy Spirit had been given on a Sunday was probably also an important factor. There may also have been a practical element. If some of the Christians from a Jewish background were observing the Sabbath, the only time they would have been able to meet with other Christians for worship would have been either before the start of the working week on a Sunday morning or in the evening (as in Acts 20:7). There is no evidence of early Christians applying the old Sabbath rules on work to a Sunday. In fact for several centuries, the first day of the week must have been a normal working day, marked only by fellowship meetings outside work hours.

As the church grew and spread, so did the importance of meeting together. The pattern that churches all around the Mediterranean got into was to meet on a Sunday. In AD 321, the first Christian Roman Emperor, Constantine, decreed that Sundays were to be an official public holiday, on which most work was forbidden. Since then Sunday has been the normal Christian day of rest and worship.

The Jewish Sabbath and Christian Sunday

If Christians have always worshipped together on a Sunday, there have been differing views on how Sunday relates to the old Jewish Sabbath. There are two extreme positions. Some Christians have felt that at least some Old Testament rules on the Sabbath should be transferred to Sunday. For them, Sundays are solemn days of rest and devotion; reading fiction or kicking a football would definitely be out. Other Christians, however, consider that the new era that Christ brought in rendered this part of the Old Testament law as obsolete as it did the laws on diet. Sunday for them is very different from the Jewish Sabbath, and they don't see a problem in reading a novel or having a bit of a kick-around in the park in the afternoon.

In fact, there is something to be said for both sides. In a phrase, I would say that for Christians the Sabbath rules are dead but the Sabbath principles remain. So when I talk—as I do—about "observing a Sabbath," it does not at all mean that I am suggesting keeping all the Old Testament laws. I mean keeping the Sabbath principle of enjoying God's day of rest.

When do we keep God's day of rest?

One other linked question needs tackling here. Does this mean that God's day of rest for us must always be on a Sunday? No, not necessarily. For one thing, many people cannot avoid working on a Sunday; for example, those in medical professions, in the emergency services, in charge of the public utilities, and last—but not least—church staff!

If this applies to you or your spouse and Sunday is a working day, then I believe it is vital that you make sure you get another day off during the week. If it can be the same day off every week and you can get into a regular routine, then fine. If, however, that is not possible, I encourage you to arrange for a full twenty-four hour stretch off: plan it out and guard it. I will make some practical suggestions later on how to do this.

The important thing is that we all need to inject into our lives a regular weekly break, whether on Sunday or on some other replacement day. But before I look at how we are to use that day, I feel it is important to look at the whole issue of work first. This commandment says something about that too.

THE BLESSINGS OF WORK AND REST

I want to make two suggestions here with regard to work and rest. The first is that we thank God for work. The second is that we take God's designated day of rest seriously.

Thank God for work

A key feature of this commandment is that it upholds the goodness and privilege of work. Yes, we are told to take one day of rest a week, but the clear assumption is that we will spend the other six days in productive work.

There is a distinction between work and employment. Employment implies a paid position, while work is something you can have and not be paid for. Many people work very long and anti-social hours to care for children or families. Yet these jobs (surely the most valuable of all) are unpaid.

We read that Adam was given work to do in Eden (Gen. 2:15) before he and Eve broke God's commands and were punished. Work was part of God's good design for humanity. Only after the calamity of humanity's fall into sin do we find that work became burdensome (Gen. 3:17–19). The fact is that human beings were designed to work.

Despite the negative press that work has and continues to have, those of us who are in employment need to thank God for it. I know that in some work situations the idea of thanking God for our job can, at best, raise a grim smile. Let me say two things. First—and I am not being flippant—I urge you to count your blessings. There have been many times in British and American history when large-scale unemployment has been common and, in some places, it still is. Second, can I encourage you to work at trying to thank God for your work? I believe that the general rule is that not only should we be working but that our work should be a positive and good thing for us. Does that phrase "a positive and good thing" describe your current attitude to your work?

One thing you may find helpful is to remember that whatever you are doing at work you are doing for God. Writing to the Colossian church, Paul gives the following instructions to—of all people—slaves: "Work willingly at whatever you do, as though you were working for the Lord rather than for people. Remember that the Lord will give you an inheritance as your reward, and that the Master you are serving is Christ" (Col. 3:23–24 NLT).

Taking such an attitude is actually possible. Brother Lawrence, a seventeenth-century cook in a French monastery, had it. He learned to bring a devotional attitude into virtually every action of his day. This enabled him to find not only meaning but also purpose in all his work. He wrote in *The Practice of the Presence of God*:

> I turn my little omelette in the pan for the love of God. When it is finished, if I have nothing to do, I prostrate myself on the ground and worship my God, who gave me this grace to make it, after which I arise happier than a king. When I can do

nothing else, it is enough to have picked up straw for the love of God. People look for ways of learning how to love God. They hope to attain it, I know not from how many different practices. They take much trouble to abide in his presence by varied means. Is it not a shorter and more direct way to do everything for the love of God, to make use of all the tasks one's lot in life demands to show him that love, and to maintain his presence within by the communion of our heart with his? There is nothing complicated about it. One has only to turn to it honestly and simply.

We all need to have some of that attitude to our own work.

Now before moving on, let me make an important point. I have been anxious here to defend work in general. That does not mean I am saying that every job is fine and all you need to do is just thank God for it. There are some jobs that are wrong, perhaps because they involve dubious practices or because they are producing things or services that the world doesn't need. Equally, there are some jobs that are good but which may be wrong for you. I can hardly tackle all the issues raised by that here. All I can say is this: Give your job its best and pray for those you work with. Thank God for whatever you can about your job and seek guidance about a way forward.

I believe it is God's will that we all have jobs that are fulfilling. But I should warn you: his idea of what is a fulfilling job may not be quite what we had in mind.

Taking rest seriously

If this commandment shows us something of the value of work, it also allows us to see the value of rest. The problem is that we tend to consider work as being important and rest as being trivial. We can think of rest as merely "not working." I want to point out that a day of rest is far more than that.

At the most basic level, a day off every week is good for us physically and mentally. It gives us the opportunity to relax the pace at which our body's machinery is working. We can rest eyes strained by computer screens, ease backs stressed by office chairs, or give a break to metabolisms kept going on caffeine. A day off may help to reenergize us, to the point that we work at a higher level of efficiency on subsequent days.

A day of rest is also important because it enables us to assess what we are doing. The problem with continuously working is that there is no opportunity to stand back, get things into perspective, and see the big picture. Deadline after deadline forces us to focus on immediate crises rather than the overall design of our lives. Many people today have a work style that is reminiscent of some racing cyclist, head down and pedaling furiously along the road. A day of rest allows us to stop pedaling, sit down, look around, pick up the map, and determine where our efforts are taking us. I have often found that it is when I am recharging, away from the place of my restless "doing," that I discover what exactly it is that has to be done.

William Wilberforce (1759–1833), who will be remembered in British history as the MP who after decades of labor brought forward legislation to ban slavery, knew the truth of this. Wilberforce was a committed Christian and never felt it right to work on a Sunday. Within a few years as a politician, he had made a great impression and was being tapped for a high position in the cabinet. The atmosphere around Westminster at the time was heady, and Wilberforce felt flattered that his hard work was on the point of being rewarded. However, after resting during the following Sunday, his view of his possible promotion changed, and he was able to write in his diary that "these earthly things assume their true size." His day of rest had given him a sense of perspective. Later in life, he was to write sadly of his contemporaries who had broken under the pressure of politics, "With peaceful Sundays, the strings would never have snapped as they did from over tension."

Taking a day of rest also makes a statement about who we are and who runs our lives. It deliberately dethrones work from being central to our existence. In the passage in Genesis 1 that this commandment refers back to, we read how, as God made everything, he stopped and stood back and saw "that it was good." Even on the ultimate job of making the entire cosmos, God does not become work obsessed. We who are made in his image would do well to learn the same principle.

In Leo Tolstoy's short story "How Much Land Does a Man Need?" a man travels to a tribe in the Russian hinterland. Villagers there offer to give him as much land as he can cover in one day. Anxious to cover as much ground as he can, the man makes a frantic journey. As the sun sets, he collapses with exhaustion and dies. Ultimately, the amount of land that he actually gets is the six-foot plot that is his final resting place.

Work becomes an end in itself, a way to escape from family,

from the inner life, from the world. Workaholism is literally fatal. Its toxic fruits are heart disease, hypertension, depression, and more. In Japan, *karoshi* or "death from overwork" is the second largest killer of working males and accounts for 10 percent of Japan's death rate. Like other addictions, workaholism consumes the addict's time, energy, and thoughts.

Forcing ourselves to take a break is also helpful because it reminds us of our limitations. We tend to think that we are indispensable in the great scheme of things. All too frequently this is an illusion. We love to be busy and to be needed, and there is no greater boost to our egos than to think that we personally hold everything together. However, making ourselves take a step away from the action can give us a healthy sense of proportion.

Yet despite all the virtues of a day of rest, for many people it is something that is just too risky. "How would I survive?" they ask. That we can trust God to provide for us if we keep his commandments is one of the lessons that the people of God learned just before Moses was given the Ten Commandments. After the Israelites crossed the Red Sea, they journeyed through the desert of Sinai. Faced with insufficient food, they made their needs known to God. In response, he miraculously provided manna for them, a substance that appeared like dew in the morning and that was "white like coriander seed, and it tasted like honey wafers" (Ex. 16:31 NLT). With the manna came strict instructions: for five days they were to collect only what they needed for that day, and if they tried to collect more it would rot and be full of maggots by the next morning. On the sixth day—the day before the Sabbath—they were told to collect twice as much, because on the Sabbath itself none would be given.

The manna of the sixth day stayed fresh and did not rot, and on the Sabbath they were able to eat what they had stored. The lesson they learned from this was that God would provide for his people in every way and that they were not going to suffer for keeping his day of rest. This is a lesson God is still trying to teach us today!

MAKING GOD'S DAY OF REST SPECIAL

In this section I want to give some guidelines on how we can get the most benefit from God's day of rest.

Guard your rest

Paradoxically, you may need to work hard to keep God's day of rest special. A day of rest does not just happen; the phone will not suddenly stop ringing just because you have decided to take a day off. You need to make a definite effort to make a day of rest and to take care to guard it. This is particularly a problem if your day of rest is not on a Sunday; everybody will assume that you are working. You will need to take positive and proactive action to make sure that your much-needed Sabbath rest is not shattered by interruptions.

It is interesting that Jesus, in the midst of a busy ministry, was proactive in taking rest. We often read in the accounts of his life how he went to a solitary place in order to escape the crowds. Sometimes he took his closest friends to be with him, and at other times he went on his own. There are lessons there for us about making firm resolutions to ensure that we do have rest.

Some of the actions we can take to guard our days of rest are concrete, physical ones. For example, if you can, divert phone calls somewhere else and refuse to check your e-mail. Make the rules you have for your day of rest widely known to others, and if you have responsibilities, try to get someone else to deputize for you.

There are other, less-obvious actions that we can take to enhance the benefit of our days of rest. If you are a news addict, then give the radio and TV a break. If doing personal administration leaves you anxious, then postpone paying bills. Don't try to tackle household tasks that will leave you drained. You may want to discipline yourself not to talk, or even think, about a nagging work situation or project.

Resolve to guard your rest. Unless you do, pressures will inevitably erode it. The time to relax is when you don't have time to relax!

Be refreshed in your rest

The Sabbath is to be a day of physical nonproductivity, a day to rest and recharge our bodies. Resting is about recovering from the week that has been; recharging is about getting ready for the week to come. One doctor said, "The periods of rest I prescribe for my patients are often Sabbaths in arrears."

Make the most of your day of rest. Force yourself to do things that are not stressful. If you don't have young children you might want to sleep in a bit longer. Find out what makes you relax and do it. In our household we often relax with a film or food. Other people like to listen to music or read a book. Many people have found that they feel refreshed by the beauty of God's creation and are especially aware of God by lakes or rivers and in woods or gardens.

You also need to monitor your Sabbath during a period of time to make sure you are getting the most from it. Do you feel better as a result? Are there ways that you could make it of greater benefit to yourself? Are there things that you do on your day of rest that are stressful? Some people who are very committed to working hard can bring the same dedication into their hobbies and sports. The result is a new area of stress. If this is you, ask yourself some hard questions. Does it really matter if you don't break your personal record for the marathon? Do you need to remodel all of the garden? Is it really relaxing to learn Chinese?

You need to be blessed by your rest: Make sure that you are.

Have freedom in your rest

One of the extraordinary abilities of the human race is that of being able to totally mess things up. You would have thought that a simple divine ruling about having a day of rest would be hard to damage. However, with perverse ingenuity, generations of people from all sorts of cultures have managed to turn this command from being a liberating gift of God into a wearisome day-long obstacle course. As I have mentioned, this happened at the time of Jesus to an extraordinary extent. The religious leaders had created a whole list of things that must not be done on the Sabbath. You couldn't prepare a meal, sew on a button, light a fire, or walk more than three thousand feet from your home. There were, in total, 1,521 of these rules, all of them inventions of the human mind, to prevent this commandment being broken. Ensuring that no work took place on the Sabbath had become very hard work!

What happened with Jesus and the Sabbath is fascinating. Time and time again his actions brought him into trouble and open conflict with the religious leaders. Jesus felt free to heal, pick grain, and cast out demons on the Sabbath. These were all actions that, in the opinion of the religious leaders, broke their rules on what could be done on the Sabbath. The fact that there were so many controversies about Jesus breaking these Sabbath rules may suggest that they were a religious abuse that he felt very strongly about. At one point, when criticized about his lax attitude to such rules, he replied, "The Sabbath was made to meet the needs of people, and not people to meet the requirements of the Sabbath" (Mark 2:27 NLT). The religious leaders had taken a blessing and turned it into an unbearable burden.

Such attitudes can occur even today; beware of them. This commandment was given to set us free, not to enslave us. That you rest is essential; how you rest is up to you.

Enjoy others in your rest

The most important things in life aren't things, but people. Sabbaths are given so that we spend time with those we are closest to. So God's day of rest should also be used to develop and extend our relationships with friends and family. Not just in brief moments, but with quality (and quantity) time. Jewish people have the practice of gathering the family as one of the focal points of their Sabbath, and central to that family time is a shared meal. For us, as a family, one thing that helps us is our rule that the telephone will be out of bounds during a mealtime. We just ignore it: whatever it is, it can wait. This allows us to give our full attention to those nearest to us—those for whom we have primary responsibility.

Enjoy God in your rest

God's day of rest is a day to worship. It is not the only day to worship and not the only day to pray and praise, but it should be the day when we have time to focus on God and our life in him. It is a day to tune in again to God, to refocus and to reprioritize all that we do and are, in the light of the reality of God.

Normally, one part of our day of rest should involve worshipping with other members of God's family. If we can take our Sabbath rest on Sunday, then giving God the first part of the first day of every week serves to remind us that he is first in our lives. Christians have always set time aside to be together: to listen to God's Word spoken into their lives, to remember Jesus' death for them in the breaking of bread, to pray together for the world, and to praise God for his goodness. To meet with God and his people is something that serves to nourish and feed us spiritually.

"Remember the Sabbath day by keeping it holy." The Sabbath day was created holy, but God wants it to be holy to you. The Sabbath is not just about time off; it is about sacred time. Sunday does not belong to business; it does not belong to industry; it does not belong to the government. It belongs to God.

So many people now have no room for God in their thoughts, in their schedules, or in the fabric of their lives. Let me ask you this: Do you keep going along with the flow of the world and let it erode your relationship with God? Does God have a chance to look into your heart? Do you give him time to do so? If not on Sunday, then when?

Stand up for the right to rest

This commandment also includes the instruction that God's people are to ensure that their sons, daughters, servants, animals, and foreigners (visitors) also keep the Sabbath. The principle, though, is plain and very up to date: We are to do all we can to make sure that others have the right to rest too.

Now of course that is not easy in a society that is driven by "market forces" (frequently a polite synonym for greed). I have a good friend, Gary Grant, who is the managing director and owner of The Entertainer chain of toy shops. Gary knows the challenge of keeping God's day of rest. What he said to me about how he responded to the pressure for Sunday trading is so helpful that I want to share it.

> We started our business in 1981 with one shop in Amersham, and for the first two years worked exceedingly long hours, seven days a week, to build the business. In 1991 I became a Christian and then had a new set of parameters. This changed many aspects of our business, from product selection, to the way we treated our staff, to the hours that we worked, and especially Sunday trading.

> In 1994 Sunday trading became lawful, and I was really concerned about how it fitted in with my Christian belief of having a day of rest. I prayed as to whether I should open my stores on a Sunday. I was annoyed that God hadn't answered my prayers, but one night God said to me, "Gary, you've had the answer, but you've been praying for the answer 'yes.'" And to this day, I know that the bit in the Bible where God says that he will honor those who

honor him is absolutely true. I can testify that God has prospered our business as we have gone from strength to strength. We have gone from three stores back in 1991 to twenty today.

The past few years haven't been easy. Many of the sites that we would have liked to open in, we have been barred from, as the landlords are only interested in people who are doing seven-day trading. However, we have found that our staff of three hundred are pleased we are taking a stance on Sunday trading, as it gives them the opportunity to be at home with their family and their children. As the owner of The Entertainer I am in a very privileged position to be able to make the decision not to trade my business on a Sunday. We only trade for six days and our business is financially viable.

God has honored Gary's decision. If you have to make similar decisions then I am sure that God will honor them too.

THE CHALLENGE OF GOD'S DAY OF REST

Let me end this discussion of God's day of rest by pointing out to you that it represents a deep challenge. The issue that this commandment addresses is a fundamental one: Who controls our time? By keeping God's day of rest we proclaim to ourselves—and to the world—that God runs our lives. If he is Lord, he is Lord of our time.

That is why there is a battle in this area. It is not simply a question of legislation on trading hours or about cultural practices; it is about the lordship of our lives and of our culture.

I believe that we all need to follow the pattern that God has established for us. Not in some dry and wearisome ritual, but in a way that liberates us and rejuvenates us. This is not selfishness. The effects of observing the Sabbath principle are wider than just our own lives; they ripple out into wider society. As one Jewish rabbi taught, "It was not Israel that kept the Sabbath, so much as the Sabbath that kept Israel." It is true today; a society without Sabbaths is a society that is heading for trouble.

For one day a week, the Sabbath is a reminder that we are dispensable to work and the world but not to our families, community, and God. Set an example, and by your use of your precious time, show that God is Lord.

You shall not misuse the name of the LORD your God, for the LORD will not hold anyone guiltless who misuses his name.

Exodus 20:7

SO WHAT'S THE PROBLEM?

The shifting popularity of children's names is a fascinating aspect of our changing society. As this new century began, the most popular names in the United Kingdom were Jack for boys and Chloë for girls. A hundred years earlier, William (followed by John and George) was the favorite name for boys, with Mary (followed by Florence and Edith) the most popular for girls. You will have to look long and hard for any Williams, Florences, or Ediths in today's school playgrounds. Clearly there are fashions in names, just as there are in clothes and cars.

Yet names are important. We can all remember when someone who should have known our name forgot it, or when we were mistaken for someone else. We can probably remember the emotion we felt too—hurt. We feel hurt when our name is forgotten, and there is an uncomfortable sense of losing importance. We feel that we are insignificant.

In fact, we go to great lengths to protect our names. An entire branch of the legal profession exists to govern the use and abuse of names. Almost any newspaper will have an account of some court case where a newspaper, TV company, publishing house, or individual is being taken to court for libel or slander. "I need to clear my name," those involved protest. We are very protective about our names.

The reason why we are so protective is because a name stands for something. Just to mention a name will often call up a whole set of images. For example, take a name like Adolf. Even without a surname, it conjures up images of indescribable cruelty, concentration camps, and persecution. But take a name like Teresa. Especially if it's coupled with "Mother," we see good, we are full of respect and admiration. As the book of Proverbs says, "A good name is more desirable than great riches; to be esteemed is better than silver or gold" (Prov. 22:1).

It is not just our own names that we are sensitive about. I remember how at school we were warned about our conduct on the bus on the way home: when we were in school uniform, any bad behavior would bring the school's name into disrepute. We have all watched embarrassed football managers on television, trying to distance their clubs from some act of urban devastation wreaked by their drunken fans. Clearly, not only can our names be misused, but so can those of others to whom we are linked, such as schools or football clubs. This third commandment is about the disturbing fact that we can—and do—misuse God's name.

The use and misuse of God's name involves far more than matters of swearing or blasphemy. It involves a number of things that relate to who God is. And for us to understand who God is will require us to do some serious thinking.

The heart of the matter
Names are more than words

Names are not just collections of consonants and vowels. They are far more than that. They have meaning, conjure up associations of ideas and images, and have power and prestige. That power and prestige can even be transferred to a third person. I'm sure many of us can remember how we used the name of some friend in order to get into a party.

The fact that we know that authority and status can be transferred with a name is behind a lot of advertising. I have already mentioned, in discussing the tenth commandment, the hold that product names have over us. The attraction that many expensive brand names have is because of the fact that people believe that something of the power of the name is transmitted to the wearer.

For some people, and for many in other cultures, naming is still important and significant because of what the name means. In *Long Walk to Freedom,* Nelson Mandela wrote:

> Apart from life, a strong constitution and abiding connection to the Thembu royal house, the only thing my father bestowed upon me at birth was a name, Rolihlahla. In Xhosa, Rolihlahla literally means "pulling the branch off the tree," but its colloquial

meaning more accurately would be "trouble maker."
I do not believe that names are destiny or that my
father somehow divined my future, but in later years
friends and relatives would ascribe to my birth name
the many storms I have caused and weathered.

Certainly, for the people of Bible times, naming a person was a serious event. Some of the names are physically descriptive. We are told in Genesis 25 when Isaac's wife Rebekah had twins, the firstborn was red and covered in hair, while the second came out holding his brother's heel. As a result they called the first one *Esau*, which means "hairy," and the other *Jacob*, which means "he grasps the heel." Other children in the Bible were given names that didn't describe them physically but spoke about what God had done or was going to do. For example, when Hannah, a barren woman who had prayed to God for a child, was blessed with a son, she called him Samuel, meaning "God heard me." The prophets Isaiah and Hosea both gave their children names that referred to what God was going to do. The best example of all is the name Jesus: this is the Greek form of the Hebrew "Joshua," which means "the LORD saves."

The name of someone in biblical times was more than just a word that identified a person. It signified something about a person and communicated something of what they stood for; to use a name was to say who that person was. God's name is no different.

The privilege of knowing the name of God
I would love to have been in the Garden of Eden just after Adam had been given the job of naming all the animals (Gen. 2:20). It

must have been a fascinating exercise, and I wonder how he came up with all the names. It's hard enough naming a single pet, let alone countless species. Behind this charming picture lies, however, a very important point. Humanity had been given dominion over living things and the first act of this dominion was for Adam to give names to the animals and birds. Yet there was one being that Adam did not give a name to: God.

God does not let human beings name him. Why not? One reason is that God is above us, and in the Bible the inferior does not name the superior. Another reason, and it is probably related, is the fact that no human being could name God properly. We wouldn't have a clue what to call him. It is said that when Ludwig Wittgenstein, the famous twentieth-century philosopher, came to discuss the nature of God in lectures, he would bring a cup of steaming coffee into the room. He would then ask volunteers to describe the smell of coffee, a task that always proved impossible without saying something meaningless like, "It has a coffeelike smell!" Wittgenstein would then make the point that if we don't have the ability to describe accurately what coffee smells like, how on earth can we hope to describe God?

Clearly, if we were trying to name or describe God ourselves, Wittgenstein's point would be valid: We would face an impossible task. Yet thankfully this is not the case, because we read in the Bible that God has revealed both himself and his name to us. We don't have to stretch our brains to try to imagine what he is like and make up some name that we hope might do him justice. God has told us who he is and has given us his name. It is vital for us to understand that what Christianity says about God comes not from vague and fuzzy human speculations, but directly from God himself. Throughout the pages of the Bible we read that God is not a something, but a Someone: a loving, personal God who cares for us and who has chosen to make himself known to humanity.

In fact when God did reveal his name, he did it in a very personal way. In Exodus 3 we read how Moses, having fled from Egypt where the Israelites were in slavery, was looking after his father-in-law's sheep in the wilderness when suddenly he came across a bush that, although covered in flames, was not burning. From the bush, God called Moses by name. God announced that he was going to liberate his people who were in slavery and told Moses to go back to the ruler of Egypt and bring the Israelites out of captivity. When Moses, evidently unenthusiastic about his mission, protested that he wasn't up to the task, God promised that he would go with him. Moses, still reluctant, then raised another objection. "Suppose I go to the Israelites," he told God, "and say to them, 'The God of your fathers has sent me to you,' and they ask me, 'What is his name?' Then what shall I tell them?" The answer is both powerful and mysterious. "God said to Moses, 'I AM WHO I AM. This is what you are to say to the Israelites: "I AM has sent me to you"'" (Ex. 3:13–14).

Two verses later God uses a name for himself, YHWH, which is a form of I AM and which, for reasons I will explain later, is translated in most English Bibles as "The LORD." This word, effectively the personal name of God, occurs some 6,800 times in the Old Testament. Each time, it refers back to this great promise, "I AM WHO I AM."

But what does I AM WHO I AM mean? It is in fact an incredibly deep statement about God. It means something like "I am the Living One" or "I am the One who exists" or "I am the One who will be who I will be." Behind these words lies the concept of a being who is quite unlike anyone—or anything—else. God's name of I AM suggests that he is a being who is independent of everything else that exists and someone who cannot be contained. With that comes the idea of God being absolutely trustworthy and unchangeable; when he makes up his mind to do something, he will do it. Furthermore, it suggests that rather than being some remote, philosophical abstraction or a vague force, God is the one who is someone. Who that "someone" is, the rest of the Bible spells out, so that by the end of it we realize that God has said to us, "I AM your Creator, Savior, Sustainer, Leader, Protector, Healer, Helper, Judge, and Comforter."

Now in revealing his personal name, God reveals his identity to us. It is quite extraordinary that God should do this because by revealing his name to us, he leaves himself open to us misusing his name. Of course, when we read about Jesus and the cross we see that, in order to help us, God went further than this. It wasn't just his name he left open for us to abuse but the life of his own Son.

In Old Testament times, people appreciated that knowing the name of God as "I AM" was a great privilege. In fact, they treated the name with such high regard that they tried to avoid using it in speech or in prayer, just in case it was misused. When the scribes came to write out the name of God, on this safety-first principle, they never wrote it out in full, but only the four consonants. And when they did come to write the Hebrew letters "YHWH" they would wash, put on new clothes, use a new quill, write the name, and then throw the quill away. When they came to read the word aloud, rather than pronounce it they substituted the word "the LORD." In fact, so reverently did they handle this word, that we are not now completely certain what it sounded like. Although our ancestors guessed that the name was "Jehovah," scholars now think that "Yahweh" was more likely; most English Bibles stick with "the LORD." In case you are worried, its exact pronunciation is not important for us as Christians because Jesus has told us that we can address God as "Father." Actually, in many ways, the name "Jesus" has taken the place of the mysterious YHWH.

However strange and ritualistic to us, the point behind not using God's name at all was a very valid one. It was to ensure that, at all costs, this commandment to treat God's name with reverence was kept. I think it would be misunderstanding these people if we felt that their motive was fear, as if God's name was some sort of unexploded bomb that had to be handled with care. I think it was rather that they knew they had a great honor and a joyful privilege in knowing the name of God. After all, the fact that God had made himself known to his people was at the center of their existence as individuals and as a nation. They were God's people, and he was their God.

Jesus and the name of God

The coming of Jesus brought in a whole new era of knowing more about God because in Jesus, God reveals himself fully. In fact, through Jesus, God now invites us to be on first-name terms with him.

The names that Jesus bears point to what he does for us. As we have seen, the name *Jesus* means "the LORD saves," but Jesus is also called Immanuel (Matt. 1:23), which means "God with us." Together ("God for us" and "God with us") they sum up all who Jesus was and is. The result is that the awesome gulf between humanity and God that had existed since Adam and Eve is now bridged. That is why Jesus is also called a mediator (1 Tim. 2:5).

Jesus himself models how we are now to treat God's name. As an observant Jew he would have known all the rules about how God's name was to be carefully revered. Despite this, he introduced a new name for God that shocked those around him. Using the word that a young child might call his father, Jesus referred to God as "Abba." His use of this term, similar to our "Daddy," displays the intimacy and confidence of a child with a parent. Yet Jesus never played down God's majesty or holiness or signaled in any way that God's name should be treated with any less honor than it had been.

Jesus makes this plain at the very start of the model prayer that he gives his disciples as an example of how to pray. We call it the Lord's Prayer and in a modern translation it begins, "Our Father in heaven, may your name be kept holy" (Matt. 6:9 NLT). In those two phrases, Jesus perfectly balances an intimate familiarity with God with a profound sense of the honor and respect that is due to God. In Jesus, God has become accessible instead of remote. He is not just a lord, he is now also our Father in heaven. Yet these new privileges give us even more reason to honor God's name.

TREAT GOD WITH REVERENCE

In our twenty-first-century Western world, God is not treated with respect. The names of God and Jesus are used lightly, or abused everywhere. I suspect much of this is not a deliberate attempt at attacking God, it is just part of the tide of disrespect for any authority figure that has flooded almost every area of our culture. No one—and nothing—is respected now, and God is just one more target to mock. Institutions and organizations that were once looked up to and highly esteemed are now treated with scorn or cynicism.

Now there are complex reasons for all this, but the fact is that no one seems to get automatic respect any more. It is quite worrying. What is more than worrying—in fact it is profoundly disturbing—is that respect has even been withdrawn from God himself.

My wife's name is Killy. That name is, for me, most precious. Were I to hear someone pouring scorn on her name, abusing it, treating it flippantly, or using it when they were annoyed or angry, it would hurt me very much. The reason is, of course, that Killy is the person I love and respect more than any other. Such abuse would show that the person didn't really know her, have regard for her, or respect her.

My reaction can be predicted: I would be angry and try and put them right. My wife deserves respect. I am sure that I am not alone in having such attitudes and responses. Now, if this is true in our relationships to other human beings, how much more should it be true for how we relate to Almighty God?

Let me give you three reasons why you should respect God's name.

Respect God's name because of his actions

God deserves respect because of what he has done and continues to do. The Bible tells us that God is the creator of the universe and that he continues to sustain it moment by moment. If God stopped his actions for even a fraction of a second, then in that brief moment of time everything—all the stars, all the cells in our bodies, every atom and molecule—would vanish into nothingness. There would just be nothing, nothing at all. When we think of that, we should realize that God is worthy of the highest respect and honor that we can manage.

God makes a similar point, only using pictorial language, in the book of Job. Job has suffered greatly; everything and almost everyone he has loved and enjoyed has been taken away from him. Although Job keeps his faith in God, eventually he comes to the point where he complains to God about the unfairness of his suffering. He demands answers. God's reply comes with thunder:

> Who is this that questions my wisdom with such ignorant words?
>
> Brace yourself like a man, because I have some questions for you, and you must answer them.
>
> Where were you when I laid the foundations of the earth? Tell me, if you know so much. Who determined its dimensions and stretched out the surveying line? What supports its foundations, and who laid its cornerstone as the morning stars sang together and all the angels shouted for joy? (Job 38:2–7 NLT)

Respect God's name because of his power

Think of the power of the most common name, Mom. The children are in their bedroom playing and all of a sudden there is screaming and crying. What happens next? One of them will come running out and cry, "Mom, Mom, he just keeps hitting me!" And Mom says,

"You go and tell your brother that I said to stop fighting." Then the child will run back, and what's the first thing you hear? "Mom said …" The child has gained power. How? By using Mom's name. How much more power exists in God's name.

In the Bible, we are told there is power in God's name. Not power in any magical sense, but because behind the name stands the one who is all-powerful, all-seeing, and all-knowing. God is the one who started the entire creation, who holds it all together, and who will, one day, reshape it. God has power over all things: over the laws of nature, over life, and over death.

God's name has power and should be revered. Calling on his name brings salvation: "everyone who calls on the name of the Lord will be saved" (Acts 2:21). In God's name evil is rebuked, in his name healing is given, in his name acts of service are done and in his name people are commissioned and sent out for service. His name should be treated with reverence. One day it will be. In the future, we are told, at his name "every knee should bow … and every tongue confess that Jesus Christ is Lord" (Phil. 2:10–11).

Respect God's name because of his character

It is not just God's actions and awesome power that should make us cautious about misusing his name; it is also his character. We worship God not just because he is powerful (after all, a dictator may have power), but because God is perfect and holy. What we find admirable in other people (their love, wisdom, and thoughtfulness) we find in God to an unlimited extent. People may sometimes be kind, truthful, and holy, but God is always love, truth, and holiness.

All human beings are, to a greater or lesser extent, sinful. If our names are misused then we may well deserve it. There may even be some truth in some of the things that are said about us. But with God there can never be any grounds for misusing his name. God is free from sin and full of everything that is good and right.

To misuse God's name is foolish because of his mighty power; it is also immoral because of his perfect character.

How to honor God's name

Let me now give you four ways in which we can honor God's name.

Don't swear

If you are anything like me, the first thing you think about when you think of this commandment is swearing. In my dear friend Dr. R. T. Kendall's book on the Commandments, *Just Grace,* he points out that in the ninth edition of The Concise Oxford Dictionary (published in 1995) the entry under the word *Jesus* is as follows: "Jesus: Colloquial interjection. An exclamation of surprise, dismay, etc. [name of founder of Christian religion d. c. AD 30.]"

In other words, *Jesus* is to be understood first as a common expletive and only then as the name of the founder of Christianity. In this environment, I think the majority of us have just become numb to the way that God's name is so widely abused in our society.

Let me suggest some ways we can counter this. First, we can watch our own language and make sure that we don't use God's name in a way that is dishonoring. Second, we can be prepared to take people to task for it. For instance, if I hear someone reply to a question with "God knows!" I often respond with something like

"Yes, he does, actually." If people say "Jesus!" as a swear word I will often ask "Who?" or "So you know my best friend, do you?" It may even be that their realization that you take God and Jesus seriously may open the door to a very interesting conversation. Third, we can let our voice be heard about the misuse of God's name in the media, especially on radio and television. A letter or a phone call is treated with quite some weight in these media organizations, and if you see or hear something that offends you, then let them know. You might point out that we are only demanding equal treatment with Muslims; after all, no scriptwriter would use the word Muhammad as a swear word!

Decide today not to use the name of God in an irreverent, frivolous, and disrespectful way.

Don't name-drop with God

This commandment addresses far more than open blasphemy, and there are ways even those who would never dream of swearing can break this commandment.

One subtle temptation is to name-drop with God. Now namedropping is perhaps one of the commonest human traits. We let people know, either openly or in a more understated way, that we know X as a friend, and we imply that he or she values our friendship. X may be a politician, a film star, a sports personality, a novelist, or even, if we are desperate, a preacher. Now when we do this with human personalities we merely make ourselves look foolish and expose our insecurity, but when we do it with God we run far greater risks.

Misusing God's name this way has been distressingly common at a national level. In history there have been far too many "holy crusades," "sacred struggles" and "wars in defense of Christian values." God has been used to justify apartheid in South Africa, death camps in Nazi Germany, and under such titles as "our mission to bring civilization," any number of greedy imperialistic ventures. Such things are not in the past: God's name was invoked on both sides in Northern Ireland. To invoke God or Christianity to enable us to oppress, intimidate, hurt, or exploit others surely involves a breach of this commandment. Those who do this will have to give an account of their claims. We would do well to learn from President Lincoln's wisdom. Shortly after the fall of Atlanta during the American Civil War, a woman exclaimed to President Lincoln at a White House function, "Oh, Mr. President, I feel sure that God is on our side ... don't you?" "Ma'am," replied Lincoln solemnly, "I am more concerned that we should be on God's side."

This sort of abuse can also occur with us as individuals and even within churches. We can use God's name to make us look good or to further our own projects. We name-drop God to give ourselves the ultimate credibility, sometimes allowing God's name to confidently underwrite something that is no more than a hunch or wish of ours. We can do it on a personal level and justify the end result with such words as "The Lord showed me that ..." The problem is that sometimes statements like this may be true; God may have spoken to us as an individual or to us as a church. But he may not, and there is often a temptation to bring him in to justify some plan that we have (especially when it needs a helping hand).

Please do not misunderstand me: I am not saying that God does not speak today. That would contradict the Bible and does not honor his name. I believe that God speaks to the church, he speaks to me as an individual about my life and work, and I believe he speaks through other Christians too. Yet I do not think that we should immediately believe everything that is claimed as being from God. Both as individuals and churches we must realize the seriousness of claiming that God has given us something specific for a situation or person. This is particularly so when the vision or prophetic word is likely to have significant implications for the person concerned.

The apostle Paul is helpful in this area. In his first letter to the church at Corinth he distinguishes clearly between what is his own advice and what he knows is from God. So in 1 Corinthians 7:10 he says, "To the married I give this command (not I but the Lord)," and then two verses later he says, "To the rest I say this (I, not the Lord)." Elsewhere he emphasizes the need for discernment: "Do not put out the Spirit's fire; do not treat prophecies with contempt. Test everything. Hold on to the good. Avoid every kind of evil" (1 Thess. 5:19–22).

Normally, when you take someone else's name and use it for your own ends, it is called forgery. When, either unconsciously or consciously, we attach God's name to something he has not said, it is as if we were writing a check and forging God's signature on the bottom. Because God makes promises, he is not pleased when we invent promises that he has not written and pass them off as his.

Don't cheat God of his honor

Strangely, we can misuse God's name by not mentioning it at all. All too often, when we do something praiseworthy, we receive all the honor. This is sadly true even if it is in answer to prayer. Often God doesn't even make it into the credit list of our lives. If the temptation we considered previously was to say that God did something that he didn't, this is the opposite: It is the temptation to say that God didn't do something, when he did.

We can honor God by crediting him with all that he does. To do this requires the much-neglected virtue of humility. Humility means that when it comes to any sort of award ceremony, we step back and wave God forward into the spotlight. After all, everything we have, we have been given by him. Even what we are inclined to think of as our own talents are nothing of the sort: they have been given to us—or more properly loaned to us—by God himself. Humility is to receive praise and to pass it on to God untouched.

Again the apostle Paul can teach us a lot. Not long after the church at Corinth was founded, some men who considered themselves superapostles began to trouble it. By boasting of what they were and what they had done, they were able to exert a harmful influence. In 2 Corinthians Paul addresses this problem and actually boasts of his sufferings. At one point (2 Cor. 12:1–7) Paul talks about "a man I know" who had the most extraordinary vision of heaven, seeing things that "no one should tell of." The odd thing is that a couple of times Paul lets slip that it was him, but because he is trying to be humble, he tells it as if it wasn't him. He goes on to say that actually he prefers to "boast about my weaknesses, so that the power of Christ may work through me" (2 Cor. 12:9 NLT). In some circles it is all too common to hear people boasting of the wonderful visions and experiences they have had, as if they had earned them. In contrast, Paul had a stunning vision but then refused to talk about it and instead changed the topic to his own weaknesses! Paul was anxious that God should get the glory, and in this he was honoring God's name, not his own.

How do we get attitudes like Paul's so that we give glory where glory is due? The best antidote to the misuse of God's name is to ensure its proper use, and the best way of using God's name properly is through praise and prayer. This is not the place to talk in detail about how we worship God, but I believe that if our worship was more God-centered the temptation to break this commandment would be drastically reduced.

There is a danger today that our worship revolves around us, when its true focus should be God. There is wisdom in the story of two people who were coming out of church, and one asked the other how they had found the service. "Oh," came the reply, "I didn't get anything out of the worship." "I'm sorry," was the response. "I didn't realize it was for you."

In this matter of not cheating God, let me ask you to review those things that you are most proud of; the things that you count as your achievements. Are you giving God adequate credit for all he has done and is doing? Have you ever thanked God for them? Do you feel that in these areas you have given him the honor that's due to him? If not, why not do it now?

Can I also ask you to review your present spiritual life? When you pray, are your prayers God-centered? Or are they self-centered? Believe me, these are hard questions for all of us, but if we are going to take this command seriously we need to respond to them. We honor God by crediting God with all that he does and is. By stealing glory for ourselves we break this commandment.

Don't live an inconsistent life

Finally, we can dishonor God's name without ever speaking a word. In fact, our words can be excellent: they can be free from swearing or any name-dropping of God, yet we can still dishonor God if the lives we live do not match up to the words we speak. We need to live lives that show that the words we say are true. Now that's difficult, but it is essential. One reason, I believe, why the church's reputation has suffered lies here. Too many people have heard "religious" people say one thing and then seen them do another.

When Jesus ascended to heaven his followers on earth became his body and continued his work and witness. Very soon they became known by his name, as Christians. Interestingly, it does not seem this was a name that they gave themselves. Instead, outsiders—who saw how central Jesus Christ was to what these people did and said—decided that *Christian* was a good term for them. His followers bore his name then, and they still do.

Now as Christians who carry this name, we are called to live lives that are worthy of the name of Jesus. It is as if we go through life with his name marked on us. Often Paul encourages us to be worthy; of some false believers he says, "They claim to know God, but by their actions they deny him" (Titus 1:16). We are urged not to bring disrepute on the family name by our behavior. We must always ask ourselves whether there is a gap between our beliefs and our actions.

In closing, there is one more thing that I feel needs to be said. It is that the whole issue of names is at the heart of our relationship with God. In Jesus, as I said earlier, we can be on first-name terms with God. Jesus in turn tells us that God cares for us so much that he knows every detail of who we are. Yet this is just the beginning of the relationship, for the amazing thing that happens when we begin to honor God's name is that he honors us back. The nearer we draw to him, the closer he comes to us. The more we call him by name, the more we hear him calling us by name. As we do this, we learn one of the most wonderful truths about God: You can never out-give him, and you can never outlove him. To honor God's name is to put in process a chain of events that, one glorious day, will result in us seeing God face-to-face.

You shall not make for yourself an idol in the form of anything in heaven above or on the earth beneath or in the waters below. You shall not bow down to them or worship them; for I, the LORD your God, am a jealous God, punishing the children for the sin of the fathers to the third and fourth generation of those who hate me, but showing love to a thousand generations of those who love me and keep my commandments.

Exodus 20:4–7

SO WHAT'S THE PROBLEM?

A confused world

Our voyage into the Ten Commandments has taken us a long way. We started by looking at coveting, lying, stealing, adultery, and murder; topics that deal very much with how we relate to our neighbors and those around us. We then came to the command to honor our parents, with all its implications for family life. Then we examined those commandments that focus not on those we meet or are related to, but on God himself. At first it was indirect, as we looked at how we remember God and look after ourselves by keeping a Sabbath. Then, more directly, it was how we honor God's name. Now, as we come to the heart of the Commandments, we will be focusing more and more on who God is. When we examine the first command-ment, we will face the awesome glory of the nature of the one true God. This second commandment deals with a vital and related issue: not so much who God is, but who God is not.

Clearly there has been a decline in traditional or institutional Christianity in Britain and America. With some splendid excep-tions, church attendance is in decline and knowledge of Christianity is limited. A generation ago, the idea of doing what I have been doing, teaching people about the Ten Commandments, would have been strange because they were part of the fabric of our society and even if we didn't keep them we were familiar with them. Now it is a strange idea because most us don't have a clue what they are!

Yet it is not as though we have moved to being an agnostic or atheistic society; religion is alive and well in our modern world. Two trends are important. The first is that we now have sizeable Muslim, Sikh, and Hindu populations. These represent what we can call for-mal religions with their own traditions, structures, and rituals.

A second phenomenon is the rise of what is generally sum-marized under the phrase "New Age religion." Akin to a spiritual shopping mall of a thousand beliefs, New Age is hard to classify. Apart from where it grades into Hinduism or Buddhism, New Age is a very informal belief; after all, one of its attractions is that you can do what you want. Whether it's meditation, feng shui, Gaia, reincarnation, astrology, crystals, tarot, or rebirthing, it's all on offer today, and you can pick and mix to suit yourself.

The arrival of other formal religions and the spread of New Age beliefs, in a situation where the church was weakened after a century of conflict about issues of philosophy, evolution, and other matters, has produced a confused and misty religious landscape. In the spiritual haze, I think three linked features stand out.

The first is the widespread rejection of any sort of authority in the religious area. "I'll believe what I want," people say proudly. Eighty-five percent of the population might well say they "believe in God," but if you asked them to describe the God they believe in, the answers would be as varied and different as the people you asked. The fact that the Bible speaks with authority on such matters really does not make it—or Christians who believe it—popular.

A second feature is the preference for spiritual beliefs that are undemanding. Religion today is presented as some sort of lifestyle option, like keeping fit or gardening. It is simply the "spiritual dimension" to life; if you need fulfillment, then you tack some spirituality on. In the supermarket of New Age beliefs, the big sellers are the packets that have on them "low in moral demands."

A third feature of modern religion is the widespread belief in the sort of tolerance that wants nothing to be ruled out. "It may not be for me," people say, "but we'd better not knock it." This goes for beliefs and for morals. One of the few New Age commandments is "Thou shall not say 'thou shall not.'" The thing that irritates such people about Christianity is not so much what it affirms but what it denies.

In fact, today we prefer to make God in our own image. Now, the thing that defines God is me; I can create a god as I would want him (or her, or it) to be. The writer G. K. Chesterton said, "When people stop believing in God they don't believe in nothing, they believe in anything." We now worship anything that suits us. The problem is that this "anything" is idolatry.

Idolatry today

I think that one of the biggest dangers surrounding idolatry is the screen of preconceptions that prevents us from seeing what it really is. When we think of idols and idolatry, our minds conjure up pictures of statues in exotic Far Eastern temples. For most of us, bowing down to some carved piece of wood or stone seems illogical, unattractive, and rather ridiculous. We smile at the thought. "No," we say. "That's one commandment you will never see me breaking!"

Idols do not have to be figures made of stone or precious metal; they do not have to be things that you can touch and hold at all. In fact, I suspect that some of the most powerful idols exist only in the mind. Human understanding is a workshop where idols are continually being crafted. Idolatry has always been around, and it always will be. The only thing that changes is the nature of the idols.

What is an idol? There are so many idols and they are so subtle that a simple definition is hard. Let me try to express it this way. A Christian could make the following statements:

- God gives purpose, meaning, and fulfillment to my life.
- God governs the way I act.
- God is the focal point around which my existence hangs.
- God is often in my thoughts, and I get enthusiastic about God.
- Thoughts of God comfort me when I am down.

- I read about God, I talk about God, I make friends with those who are also committed to God.
- I desire more of God.

You've got the picture? Now idolatry is where something—anything—takes the place of God in this central position. An idol is anything that you could put in place of the word *God* in statements like those above. Try it with "money," "possessions," "careers," "holidays," "sports," "music," "sex," "relationships," or almost anything else. That is what an idol is. An idol is what people live for. An idol is what fills our minds when we lie awake at night; idols are what we buy magazines about; idols are what we spend our time, money, and energy on. Idolatry occurs when we hold any value, idea, or activity higher than God.

The heart of the matter

Let me raise two questions. Why are we so prone to idolatry? Are idols that bad anyway? I believe that if we can answer these questions, we will have come a long way to understanding the problem of idolatry.

The attraction of idolatry

Idolatry, it seems, is a universal feature of the human species. Yet why is it so attractive?

The first thing to say is that idols are not basically evil. In fact, the most dangerous idols are actually good things that have been twisted. Think of the things I just listed as being potential idols. Not a single one of them is bad—they are all good, and all gifts from

God. And as good things they retain their attraction for us. In fact, the very best things make the most tempting idols.

Let me give an example of how this works with one very dangerous modern idol: nationalism. Now God made different peoples, ethnic groups, and races. God obviously appreciates diversity, and he delights in such differences. I also have no doubt it is a good thing to celebrate our culture, to love our nation, and to be proud of it. Yet it is all too easy for those attitudes to slide over into something far nastier. If the race or the nation that we belong to starts to become the central feature in our lives, then we must be careful. Once we start saying that we are better than our neighbors, or that any means justifies us beating them in sports or business, then we are in trouble. It is not hard to see where nationalism can lead you: you only have to look at Hitler's Germany or Rwanda or the Balkans.

The other attraction of idolatry is that idols are generally tame gods that you can keep at arm's length. For one thing, they make fewer moral demands on us than the real God. The one true God is so uncompromising that idols present something of an attractive alternative.

The classic example of the attractions of idolatry can be found in the Bible. Even as God was giving this commandment to Moses on Mount Sinai, the Israelites were breaking it. Why? Moses, we are told, had been up the mountain for some days and the people were frustrated and impatient with waiting for God. They wanted something instant and immediate. So Aaron melted down their jewelry, cast it into a golden calf, and presented it to the people as a substitute focus for their worship. The attraction of idols is not that they are gods; it is that we know they are not gods. Idols offer the possibility to men and women of making their own controllable god—one they can deal with on their terms.

It is not wise to underestimate the subtle attraction of idols. The story of King Solomon is very sobering. He was the wisest man of his day, a zealous and pious constructor of the temple, and a man whom God had appeared to twice (see 1 Kings 3—10). Yet we read in 1 Kings 11 how in his old age he turned to the worship of foreign gods and incurred God's anger. If a man like Solomon can fall into idolatry, then you and I ought to be very careful.

The adultery of idolatry

"But so what?" I hear people say. "Does it matter that our culture is awash with a thousand varieties of formal and informal religion? Does it matter that for many, football, shopping, or films are what is at the heart of their lives?"

With regard to these other religions and beliefs, I can imagine people saying: "Well, isn't God big enough to handle this? Does God really mind whether he is called 'Krishna,' 'Gaia,' or 'Great Light of the Cosmos'? And if people worship rocks, trees, or crystals does it really matter? I mean, no one's perfect. Besides shouldn't the church (and God) be glad of any devotion, whatever form it may take?" I can hear people protest that surely God doesn't mind if our hobbies, causes, and pursuits are the core of our lives. After all, he made these things. God can't seriously be threatened by someone's love of a garden, fishing, or sports.

To answer these questions I want to go back to the seventh commandment (see how they all are related?) and talk about adultery.

I love my wife, Killy, very, very much. We were married in 1983, and I am more in love with her today than when we married. But can you imagine how she would feel if, finding my wallet on my desk, she noticed a photo of another woman alongside the one that I have of her? Do you think that she would say, "Well this is interesting, but my husband is entitled to his freedom and privacy, so I won't ask any more"? Don't you think it far more likely that she would immediately find me and demand to know who this other woman was and what her picture was doing in my wallet? What do you imagine her reaction would be if she learned that I had developed a friendship with this woman outside of our marriage and that I turned to her when I felt especially in need of support, affection, or encouragement? Could you blame her if she confronted me, tore the photograph into pieces, and demanded that I never see the other woman again? Could you fault her for feeling jealous, hurt, betrayed, and angry about having to share my love and devotion with another?

These are obviously absurd questions. You can't love a person and be tolerant of other loves. You can't love someone and be indifferent about that person having an affair. Killy is my wife; she has every right to expect and insist that I keep myself for her and her alone. And I want to live up to those expectations, because I love her, I need her, and our relationship is the most important earthly thing I have. And the idea that there might be "someone else" is terrible to both of us. Yet a scenario like this goes to the heart of the issue that is addressed in this commandment.

In fact, this commandment is about how we love God, a relationship for which the nearest parallel we have is marriage. In marriage, there is no room for any other person, precisely because a marriage is totally based on a unique and exclusive relationship between two people. That exclusivity is at the very heart of what a marriage is all about. And our relationship with God is to be similar.

Both are personal relationships that are bound by pledges of faithfulness and priority. In fact, the concept of a covenant, a mutually binding treaty of one party to another, lies at the heart of both relationships. As the husband and wife make promises exclusively to each other, so God and his people make similar promises; he to protect and bless us and we to trust and obey him. A key element of any covenant, ancient or modern, is its restricted nature; it is only between the named parties. The exclusivity that is at the core of a marriage is also at the heart of our relationship with God.

Now idols are those things that tempt us away from our exclusive bond to God. They strike at the very foundation of this relationship with him by introducing someone else. God is as uncompromising about the purity of his relationship with us as any partner in a marriage—in fact even more so. In the Bible, he uses strong language about what bringing any idols into this relationship means. It is adultery, unfaithfulness, a breaking of a sworn agreement, the very deepest breach of trust and devotion. In short, God wants sole rights to our worship.

Confronting idolatry today

I want now to look at how we combat idolatry. First, I want to give you some signposts on strategy, and then I want to look at some specific areas where idolatry needs to be confronted today.

How to confront idolatry

Recognize a double danger. Two opposite dangers exist when we recognize the power of idolatry in our lives.

The first danger is that of simply giving up. Faced with overwhelming pressure from our culture to worship such things as sex, power, and possessions, we could just shrug our shoulders in defeat. This is wrong. If we realize how serious idolatry is and how much of an affront it is to God, we cannot simply give in.

A second danger is subtler. It looks at what the idolatry centers on and rejects that. Is sex being worshipped? The response is to be against sex. Is meditation being made a god? The response is to reject anything in our own worship that remotely smacks of being contemplative. Is a sport becoming an idol? The response is to preach against it and to be suspicious of anyone in the congregation in trainers. Is being green replacing being godly? The response is to ostentatiously drive to church rather than walk.

It is easy to find ourselves trapped between these two positions of defeatism or unconditional rejection. Let me suggest a more profitable strategy.

Plant the flag for God! The theologian Dr. Tom Wright talks about a discovery he made that helps us address the question as to what we should do to confront idolatry. He tells that when the first Christians arrived in Britain and started to build places of worship, they chose to build them on sites that the pagans had used for worship. Why did they choose to build on top of places where there had been temples and shrines to pagan gods? Was it because there was something special about those places? No, it wasn't that. Rather, it was a conscious decision to say something about Christianity: that the call to us is to worship God in places where idols are worshipped. It is to plant the flag for God in hostile soil, to claim the good things of God for him, to proclaim that only under the loving and gracious gaze of God can everything be held in the right balance and with the right perspective.

I find this a very helpful concept. Instead of running away scared or seeking what we can reject because it has been contaminated by idolaters, this gives us a better alternative. Of course, it's harder work, but then most good ideas are.

Some current confrontations

With these things in mind, I want us now to look at five areas where there is a struggle against idolatry going on. This is not an exhaustive list, nor are these five necessarily the worst issues. But they make good case studies, and I believe that the principles that we see in them can be applied elsewhere.

Preserving the natural world. As I suggested earlier, as a rule the best things make the most tempting idols. It is when God's handiwork is at its best that we are most tempted to worship it instead of its creator. Nowhere is this truer than in the area of the environment.

Until almost within living memory, humanity's attitude to the natural world was straightforward. Life was a hard struggle for existence against the elements, the seasons, and predators, and pests great and small. Suddenly, in the past few decades, there has been a growing realization that our species is capable of doing permanent and lasting harm to the world. Indeed, as the ever-growing list of extinct species demonstrates, we have already done it. The result of this has been a great deal of interest in the environment—something that is good, right, and long overdue.

Yet parallel to this concern has emerged a variety of views associated with the New Age movement in which the earth, living things, and Nature (always with a capital letter) are to be worshipped. Indeed some people, digging around in old mythologies, have revived terms such as Mother Earth or Gaia for the planet and have credited her (feminine deities are currently fashionable) with being the creator. The splendor of the natural world is to us a mirror in which God's glory is reflected. The distinction is important; I know that Killy would think me very strange if I paid more attention to her reflection than to her.

So what should we do when, in this area of the environment, we see a good thing being turned into an idol? As I suggested earlier, the answer is not, I'm afraid, simply to scream "Idolatry!" and run away with our eyes closed. The solution is to "plant a flag for God" in this area. To do that means first the hard work of thinking and praying through how we should treat the natural world and, then, the even harder work of getting out there and doing it.

In fact there are an increasing number of Christians involved in conserving the environment and there are some remarkable projects underway in the name of God.

Sex. Whether in Soho's strip joints, the pages of *Playboy*, the office affair, or at a teenager's party, erotic love continues to entice us with the promise of bliss and escape. In our discussion of the seventh commandment, I talked about the effect that the worship of sex has on our society, and there is no need to go over that again here. But here is a classic case of idolatry. How do we deal with it?

Here, too, there is a temptation to adopt a simple solution and reject the good that is being abused. This has led in the past to attempts either to enforce celibacy or to deny, even in the right circumstances, the good of eroticism. Here problems arise. When sex is not talked about, sexuality soon becomes something to be wary of and kept away from. The trouble is that sexuality is too potent a force to be neutralized by simply pushing it below the surface of our lives. Out of sight, the clock on the bomb may still be ticking. Some people are so afraid of facing up to their problems in the area of sex that they try to pretend that they have no past or present struggles. This can be the recipe for future disaster.

Let's "plant the flag" for God in the area of sex as well. It will not be easy. The middle of a battlefield is never an easy place to plant any flag, and I have no doubt that both sides will misunderstand us when we try and set up God's ideal standards and claim this whole area of human life for him. We will need to be patient and gracious with those who are victims of the god of sex—an ever-increasing number of whom are cast aside, people who are hurting and need the healing of the God of life.

The body. The whole discussion on sexuality leads to another major god of our age—the perfect body. In this "feel good" age, the second commandment could read "Do not make yourself an idol." "How do I look?" has become a question that haunts both sexes, from adolescence upward. We are surrounded by examples of those who are portrayed as being physically perfect: the super-thin supermodels, the lean and muscular athletes, the glamorous and immaculately groomed rich. In a million air-brushed and digitally manipulated glossy pictures, human perfection is laid out before us. "Are you like this?" ask the advertisements. And depressed and guilty we stare at ourselves in the mirror and try to tug our waistlines in. We bow to what the scales say about us, and let their verdict determine how we feel about ourselves. It is idolatry.

On the idolatrous altar of the perfect body we pile up sacrifices of wealth, time, and health. We feel we must stave off age and its ravages at all costs, whether by beauty treatments or surgery. Low self-image is common among young people who feel that they just don't look right, and the numbers of people suffering from eating disorders like anorexia and bulimia have never been higher.

Yet when we look at this idolatry, we see again the pattern that we have seen before. Once again, it takes what God made good and fatally distorts it by making it everything. To state that one look or one physique is superior to another denies the truth that we are all made in God's image. It also hides the fact that God made us all different and that he is far more concerned about who we are than what we look like.

Yes, we would agree, healthy bodies are important, and it is good to pursue bodily health for ourselves and for others. Our bodies shouldn't be mistreated, neglected, or discarded; we are to take good care of what God has given us. However, we might gently want to point out that our bodies, even the fittest, are not going to last for ever; we are all finite and fragile. We would also want to state, very firmly, that we are all made in the image of God and given his breath of life. The God who created us values each and every one of us, whatever we look like. In fact, God loves us all so much that he put the highest value on us: the life of his Son. We would do well to remind ourselves that beautiful bodies are fine but what God seeks most of all is not outward good looks, but an inner, spiritual beauty. Only that is of eternal value.

Power. *Power* is a word that makes us sit up and listen. The media talk about global military power and economic power. We talk about power in our offices, councils, and governments. Cars and computers with ever-greater power tempt us. We read of politicians and governments "coming to power," when we had thought they were being "elected to serve." In today's world, power of every sort is important and is worshipped.

Here again we see the same pattern of the good gift mutated into the tempting idol. There is nothing wrong with power: used correctly and responsibly, much good can be done. God has given humanity power, and we are called to exercise it for the sake of his world and his people. The trouble occurs when power is pursued as an end in itself, so that it is desired just to control and influence others. This is so tempting that it is all too common for people who started off seeking power for all the right reasons to end up becoming corrupt and betraying their original principles simply in order to stay in power. Not even the church is immune from the idolatry of power. Power seems to become an idol very easily.

So how do we react? Never having power is too easy an answer. If we opt out of society, we can hardly complain when things go wrong. We are told to be salt and light in society, and to be either means that we must be where we can have influence. There are numerous examples in both the Old and the New Testaments of men (Daniel, Ezra) and women (Esther) who used their power for good, even within corrupt systems.

Think about how your exercise of power at home, work, or church matches up to that of Jesus, who had unlimited power on earth. Do you have the same attitude as he did? Do you have the same concern for the poor and powerless as he did? We have no excuse for worshipping power when we have the greatest possible example of someone rejecting its attractions put in front of us. Jesus totally rejected the corruption and idolatry of power. So should we.

Possessions. I talked earlier of the greatest of all our modern-day temples of worship: the shopping centers. We are a nation whose favorite pastime of shopping is in order to amass yet more possessions. This is an ancient trait in our species; human beings have always accumulated things and been strangely obsessed by them. In fact, much of what we know about the ancient world is because people were so strongly linked to their possessions that they had them placed with them in their graves.

In planting the flag here, let me sketch out some guidelines. We will have possessions, but we must hold lightly to them.

Can you look around at all that you have (house, car, DVDs, music, books, and clothes) and say, "Well, God, if you asked me to, I could give them up." If we can say that, we are on the right track. An even better practice is to get into the habit of giving things, even good things, away. Nothing insults idols quite so much as giving them away.

These are just some examples of where idolatry is being confronted. What you and I need to do is to look at our own lives and see where the idols need to be challenged. Where in your life do you need to plant the flag for God?

REMEMBER THE COST OF IDOLATRY

As we come to the end of looking at this commandment, I want to discuss the cost of idolatry.

It is worth remembering that the Ten Commandments are given for our benefit, not God's. He is against idolatry, not just because it robs him of his rightful worship but because it is hurtful to us. In this commandment, as in all the others, he has our own best interests at heart.

Idolatry is harmful in two ways. The first is that it cheats and destroys those who practice it, and the second is that it steals from us the most precious thing we can have: a knowledge of the living God.

Idolatry cheats and destroys the idolater

The whole basis of idolatry is that it is a lie. We take things that are not God and pretend that they are. The results are catastrophic. For a start, idols lie to us. Think of the examples we've just looked at:

- The idol of the natural world whispers that, if we serve it, it will show us truth and meaning and give us purpose in our lives. But it never does.
- The idol of sex murmurs to us that, if we serve it, it will give us a permanent state of ecstatic joy, delight, and intimacy. But it never does.
- The idol of the body tells us that, if we serve it, it will

make us the gods and goddesses that we want to look like. But it never does.

- The idol of power thunders at us that, if we serve it, it will give us the freedom to do whatever we want, whenever we want. But it never does.

- The idol of possessions announces that, if we serve it, it will make us fulfilled, complete, and content. But it never does.

They all lie. They never—except for the briefest moment—ever deliver. Many years ago, an Old Testament prophet said the following: "Every goldsmith is shamed by his idols. His images are a fraud; they have no breath in them" (Jer. 10:14). It is hard to argue with that summary of things.

If this was all that idols did to us, then that would be bad enough. But it gets worse. Idols also enslave their followers. In an effort to find what the idols have promised, we get lured in ever deeper. Devotees of the idol of sex know it well: They spend their lives in a futile, dangerous, and ever more draining hunt for sexual fulfillment. But that is a mirage, as real as the pot of gold at the rainbow's end. The idol of possessions exerts the same hold; you may "shop until you drop," but even then you will still want more. Idolatry is as satisfying as drinking saltwater.

The reason why idols grip us in an ever-tighter embrace is simple. When we give to some part of the created world the worship that belongs to God the Creator, that idol acquires power over us. We may think they serve us, but in fact it is totally the other way around—we serve them. And idols are cruel masters.

Some of the most profound words on idols are found in the Psalms, the worship book of God's people.

> Our God is in the heavens, and he does as he wishes. Their idols are merely things of silver and gold, shaped by human hands. They have mouths but cannot speak, and eyes but cannot see. They have ears but cannot hear, and noses but cannot smell. They have hands but cannot feel, and feet but cannot walk, and throats but cannot make a sound. And those who make idols are just like them, as are all who trust in them. (Ps. 115:3–8 NLT)

The psalm writer is making the point that the idols of men and women are not real, they are not living, and they are not lasting. They are useless.

What is more, the writer says, their makers become like them. It is hardly surprising that when people worship idols they become like them: more and more unreal, more and more untrue, more and more false, and more and more dead. The trouble with idolatry is that it makes us less than human.

Idolatry cheats us of the living God

You may not believe it possible, but there is still worse news about idolatry. It is this: Idolatry hides the fact that God wants to be the center of our lives. Around sixteen hundred years ago the wise St. Augustine opened the account of his conversion with the following statement to God: "You made us for yourself, and our hearts find no peace until they rest in you." What he was saying is that there is a "God-shaped void" in our lives that only God can fill. Idols fatally obscure that fact.

Psalm 115 said of the true God, "Our God is in the heavens, and he does as he wishes" (NLT). There is a fierce independence about God that demands respect. If there is a danger that we ignore the true God by worshipping idols instead, there is also another danger—that of treating the true God as simply another, but bigger, idol. In coming to the real God, we are coming to someone who will never be at our beck and call.

We see this idea that the living God is free, active, and cannot be manipulated again and again in the life of Jesus. There is an independence about Jesus that we can—and ought to—find disturbing. Jesus can never be controlled or made to say what we want him to say; he will never "toe the party line," and he never marches to our tune. Yes, he keeps his but in his way and in his time. He wants us to pray to him, but we can't give him orders.

Now this has exhilarating consequences for those of us who are followers of Jesus. You see, I made the point earlier that we become like the things we worship and that dead idols produce enslaved idolaters. But in contrast to the idols, God is alive and free; he does hear, does see, does feel, does speak, and does know. The Bible tells us we were made in the image of God; therefore if we worship him, we become more human, more like the people we were made to be. To worship God is to become liberated.

Oddly enough, this is something to remember especially in our churches. One of the dangers in the Christian faith can be that we acquire a certain view of God and how he works, and cling on to it.

These images or ideas are often formed through experiences or teaching. They are often good and right ideas and were probably God-given. The trouble is that we let them set the agenda for how God must work again; we hold on to past experiences and just look for repeats. We look back to wonderful times in the life of a church and use them as the criteria for whether God is working today. If something doesn't fit the pattern, then we reject it. I travel a lot and meet many people who have made past experiences, past churches, and past ways of doing things into idols. Some aspect of their faith rather than God himself has become the thing they really worship. Because of this idolatry, new and good things can be rejected. Now, of course, I am not saying that new things are always the best, or that novelty is a proof that God is working in a situation. What I am saying is that we are dealing with a God who is living, who is more real and alive than we ever imagine. We must allow God to be God and not treat him as a tame idol.

Keep yourself from idols

At the very end of a letter written as an elderly man, the apostle John wrote this, "Dear children, keep yourselves from idols" (1 John 5:21).

Let me ask you what the "photos in your wallet" are that could gradually steal you away from a relationship with God. Are there any things to which you have been offering sacrifices, perhaps secretly? What do you talk about the most? What does that reveal about the things you have at the center of your heart? How free are you to give things away or to give things up?

We must all confront these idols, because they will hold us captive if they are not confronted. And, I'm afraid to say, it will not just be us they enslave. Did you notice that this commandment talks about the children of those who bow down to idols? That is not because God is some vindictive God who wants to punish innocent people; it is because idolatry has repercussions that, unless God intervenes, roll on for years. Whole families, and generations, get taken into captivity. What the parents worship, the children will too. It is clear the stakes are high.

There is room for only one woman's photo in my wallet: Her name is Killy. There is only room for one Lord in my life: His name is Jesus. What about you? We may reject God's warning by neglecting this commandment. But as Jonah in the Bible learned the hard way, "those who cling to worthless idols forfeit the grace that could be theirs" (Jonah 2:8).

Now let me conclude with an encouragement. One of the exciting things about times like these is that we suddenly find ourselves in the world of the Bible again. The atmosphere that Christianity was born and grew up in was full of idols and worship of other gods. With great skill and courage, churches in cities and towns around the Mediterranean confronted idols and called the people to worship Jesus as Lord—as the God who was not created by them or controlled by them.

It is this call that the world needs to hear again and needs to see lived out again. The apostle Paul, when he wandered around the city of Athens just less than two thousand years ago, was "greatly distressed to see that the city was full of idols." He then proclaimed the gospel, and many turned from idols to serve the true and living God (Acts 17).

God knows that the "images" offered by the world are bankrupt. He knows that if we pursue them, in the end we will find ourselves disappointed, devastated, and worthless. The false gods will only take, take, and take. The true and living God gives, gives, and gives again.

Now, as we come to the first commandment, it is this true and living God we have the joy to consider.

You shall have no other gods before me.

Exodus 20:3

SO WHAT'S THE PROBLEM?

Finally, we have arrived at the very heart of the Commandments, the great rule that we are to have no other gods but the one true and living God. If the second commandment deals with idols, those make-believe gods, this concentrates exclusively on the true God.

Now it is this commandment that underpins all the others and is the reason for everything we have already looked at. As the sun lies at the center of the solar system and has the planets orbiting around it, so all the other commandments revolve around this first one. God himself lies at the heart of the Commandments and holds them all in place. It is vital that we understand this for two reasons.

First, it reminds us that we cannot remove God from the Commandments. This is something that people often try to do. In fact, if you think about it, I could have written a book on the Ten

Commandments following the pattern that I have adopted here, but without so far mentioning God at all. In it, I would have argued that not murdering, coveting, or stealing was a good idea because it was the best way for a stable society to exist. I could have argued that not coveting leads to less stress, having a day off a week makes you feel better, and that not committing adultery keeps your marriage intact.

I would not have been lying; in fact, all these things are correct. True, I would have to do some fast footwork on the last one. But even there, I think I could have justified a "no-idolatry policy" on plain commonsense grounds, probably by interpreting it to mean "thou shalt not get things out of proportion." Such a set of commandments would probably be very popular and might find wide support across the diverse religious and spiritual landscape of our society. But this first commandment makes such an interpretation totally impossible. These are God's Commandments and his name and character are stamped through them.

Yet as sensible as these Commandments might be, they only really make sense when we see God as being behind each of them. Murder is wrong, primarily because it takes from another person what was given them by God—life itself. Bearing false witness or lying is wrong because God is a God of truth. Adultery is wrong because God is a God of faithfulness. And so on. For us to really understand these Commands, I want to argue that it is vital we understand the God who is behind them.

Secondly, Christianity isn't just about obeying some rules for life. It is not about "the best way to act," or having a "moral code to guide us." To say that Christianity is only about keeping the Ten Commandments is like saying that driving is all about keeping the traffic regulations. No one would say that. We all know that driving is something else: it is getting into a car, starting the engine, and traveling. The traffic regulations are vital, but they are not at all what driving is about. The Ten Commandments have a similar relationship to the Christian life: They are the guidelines for life; they are not the life itself. This is something that needs to be explained because many people think that this is exactly what Christianity is. They think of it as being about a code of rules to live by. It is not. Fundamentally, Christianity is about getting and staying in a right relationship with God. And that is why this first commandment is so important. It puts God first.

The heart of the matter
Who is God?

"Very well," someone might agree, "God is behind all the Commandments. But who is this God? After all, there are many different gods around. Why should we take account of this one?"

Actually, God declares who he is at the very start of the Commandments. We mislead ourselves if we start the Commandments by simply saying, "Number one: You shall have no other gods before me." The Commandments really start with the two previous verses: "And God spoke all these words: 'I am the LORD your God, who brought you out of Egypt, out of the land of slavery. You shall have no other gods before me'" (Ex. 20:1–3).

The way the Commandments are set out is very similar to a legal or treaty agreement. They start, like most legal documents have done ever since, with the name of the one who makes the agreement. It is not quite "I, John Smith, the undersigned, do hereby …" but it is not far from it. In this brief introductory sentence, the one who makes the treaty with his Commandments sets out who he is. In it, God defines himself.

When we read these opening words carefully, we can find in them direct or indirect mentions of four descriptions of God. He is God, the maker of all things; he is the LORD, the one who reveals himself to humanity; he is King, the one who is our God; and he is Redeemer, the one who saves his people. Using these four pointers as guides, I want to sketch out briefly what the Bible tells us about the one who gave the Ten Commandments to us.

The one who creates and sustains—God

"And God spoke all these words ..." The Bible opens with the declaration that God is the maker of the cosmos, of all living things, and of us. God is the one behind all the breathtaking beauty and astounding intricacy of the world we see. He is the one who is both powerful enough to create vast star systems and delicate enough to make a butterfly's wing. All the rhythms of days and seasons, all the cycles of life with their complex interdependency that we will never get to the bottom of, are God's handiwork.

God has not finished being God, either. The Bible is plain that he continues to work in the universe by sustaining it and keeping it going. What we see as the "laws of nature" are simply a description of God's normal working patterns. In everything that happens, from the sun shining to flowers blossoming, we see God's powerful but gentle hand.

Jesus, as God made flesh, was also a creator. Without being flippant, we can say that he took after his Father in this respect. We see this in the miracles where, for example, he turned water into wine, multiplied fish and bread, and stilled storms. He did things that only a creator God could do. Perhaps we could say, though, that Jesus' main work was not so much in the area of creation but in the area of re-creation. In a world where God's good creation had been damaged, Jesus brought a healing and restoring touch: the blind had sight given them, the paralyzed were given working legs, and even the dead were raised. Now in heaven, Jesus continues that work. He creates new things, and he restores and renews things that are damaged and broken by sin. And one day, we are promised, he will return in power and restore this ravaged world and make a new creation.

Now such a view should fill us with awe and reverence, and it ought to move us to worship. It should encourage us to treat these Commandments seriously and inspire us with confidence in them. These Commandments are indeed the maker's instructions, and we would be well advised to follow them. Be sure that the only god you have is this God.

The one who reveals himself—LORD

"I am the LORD your God ..." In this opening to the Commandments, God states that he is the LORD. We looked at that strange expression "the LORD" when we discussed the third commandment. Just to remind you, it is an attempt by our English translators to represent the personal name of God that is written in Hebrew as YHWH but which was probably pronounced "Yahweh." Behind this name lies the vital truth that God is not simply a maker or creator; he is also one who reveals himself to people.

This is critical. If God had not spoken to us frail and finite people we could never have found out about him. He would have remained a distant mystery, someone—or something—who could only be speculated about. But we see throughout the Bible how God spoke repeatedly to humanity and how he has revealed to us who he is and what his character is like. In giving his name, with its links to the great statement that he is the "I AM," God is allowing himself to be found by us. As God reveals in the Bible that his name is "the LORD" or Yahweh, he also lets us know that this is his covenant name. It is this name under which he makes—and keeps—his promises to the human race.

There is a distance between humanity and God, a distance caused not just by him being the eternal, infinite God but also by him being holy and us being sinful. In Jesus, though, God reveals himself fully to us. We see in Jesus as much of God as we can take in. God is no longer elusive, appearing only rarely to the very holiest of people; he stands before us in the flesh.

In Jesus, we see what God is really like. Perhaps you've seen the film *The Wizard of Oz*? If you have, you will remember that Dorothy and her friends follow the yellow brick road and eventually get to the Emerald City to see the great wizard. There they get ushered in for an audience with him and find themselves standing in front of a huge and awesome face from which comes a booming voice. Then the yappy dog Toto pulls the curtain and reveals the real wizard: an old man who projects his face onto a big screen and speaks through a microphone. The whole thing is a fraud and a big disappointment. It's important to realize that the God of the Bible isn't like that. In Jesus, he meets us face-to-face and openly. There is no projection or screen, no booming voice or curtain.

Jesus' role in showing who God is did not end with his death, resurrection, and return to heaven. Jesus said he would never leave his people and promised that when he had gone back to heaven God would send his Holy Spirit to stand alongside believers in his place. True to that promise, God still comes to his people—now no longer a nation but instead spread worldwide as the church—in the Holy Spirit. The Spirit reveals to us his love and his care, speaks to us his truth, and helps us to pray and to know him.

The God who gave these Commandments is not a distant, aloof God. He is a God who has revealed himself to us, most fully in Jesus. He is a God who has done all he can to come down alongside us, to show us who he is, and made it as easy as he can for us to enter into relationship with him.

The one who rules humanity and history—King

"Your God." It would be easy to overlook this little expression, "I am the LORD your God." To do that would be to lose a great truth, because this phrase points to the bond or agreement that already existed between Yahweh and the people of Israel. They are his people, and he is their God. This is the language of a king and his subjects, and much of the setting and the structure of the Commandments is similar to the sort of treaty that kings made.

That God is King is a theme that occurs throughout the Bible. God, it declares, is King over humanity. He is King over individuals in that he sets laws for us, and he is King over nations in that he orders their rise and fall. He is also King over history in that he makes all its tangled events work out to serve his purposes. These Commandments were given that God himself might be King over the nation of Israel and that they would be his people. As we read in the Bible, we see that this idea was rejected by the nation of Israel, and they decided they would rather have a human and visible king than a divine but invisible one. These earthly kings failed, but the hope remained; one day the Messiah, the godly King, would sit on David's throne.

The kingship of Jesus is not yet fulfilled; he is now the hidden king over a world that still rebels against him. That will not last forever. The Bible is full of promises about the future and how, on a day unknown, Jesus will return in unspeakable glory and majesty to be the crowned ruler of this world. As he does, history as we know it will end and the kingdom of God will triumph. King Jesus will exercise a final and full act of judgment, and all those who have turned to him will live with him forever. All evil, along with all those who practiced it, will be eternally destroyed. In the new heaven and earth that the King will bring in, eternal wholeness, joy, and life will replace all the pain, mourning, and dying of this present age.

The God who is King gave the Ten Commandments, and if we are to be the King's people then we must follow them. Yet because of the fact that he is the King and because he will triumph one day, we also know that to keep his Commandments is the best possible investment for our future.

The one who saves his people—Redeemer
"Who brought you out of Egypt, out of the land of slavery." Finally, in this brief introduction to the Ten Commandments, God reminds his people that he has acted on their behalf. He is not just God the Creator, God the LORD, and God their King, he is the God who has taken them out of Egypt and brought them out of slavery there.

This is another great theme of the Bible: God is our redeemer, rescuer, and deliverer. Almost as soon as humanity had fallen into sin and rebelled, God announced that there would be a deliverer. The entire history of the Old Testament is that of God working out his purposes to create a people of his own from whom the great deliverer could come. He called Abraham and made promises to him, brought his descendants out of Egypt and put them in the Promised Land. Then through wars, famines, and exile, under judges, prophets, and kings, God taught his people that he was the one and that he would accept no rivals. God also taught them that he was holy and that the only way a sinful humanity could come to him was by rigorously and repeatedly obeying a system of animal sacrifices. Throughout these centuries of discipline and learning, God continued to show that he was a loving Redeemer, constantly reaching out to rescue his people and forgive them.

Finally, just over two thousand years ago, a baby was born into a family of the kingly line of David, in David's own city. This child, Jesus, grew up to start his ministry acclaimed as "the Lamb of God that takes away the sin of the world." Throughout his ministry of preaching and healing, he made a number of references (often misunderstood by those around him) to his death. He would, he said, "give his life as a ransom for many," have to "drink the cup" of God's judgment and wrath, and be "the good shepherd who lays down his life for the sheep." Finally, on the night of his betrayal, Jesus spelled out the meaning of his imminent death to his followers. Using the language of sacrifice, he told his followers that the broken bread and poured wine of the Last Supper represented his body and his blood.

The next day after a series of hasty sham trials, Jesus was executed on a cross. What happened there is something so momentous that it is difficult for our minds to comprehend. Somehow, in dying on the cross, the totally innocent Jesus took upon himself the guilt and sin of other human beings, and again he became the God who saves.

I rather like this rural picture I was once given of how a country fox gets rid of its fleas. It collects bits of wool from hedgerows and fences and makes them into a ball in its mouth. It then walks into a stream slowly, causing the fleas to scramble up its body. As the fox goes deeper into the water, the fleas climb towards its neck and face until the fox lowers its head under the water and all that remains above the water is the ball of wool. The fleas climb onto the wool, the fox lets go and the fleas float off down the river, leaving behind a clean fox. Jesus, in some way, acts like that ball of wool; he acts as the focus for evil, absorbing the sin of the world so that we can be clean.

It is no accident that God referred back to the way he had saved his people from Egypt before giving them the Commandments. He wanted to remind them that he was their Redeemer. We have a far greater privilege than they had. The Israelites knew merely that God had redeemed them out of Egypt. We know that, in Jesus, he has redeemed us from hell.

The one who is more than we can imagine

This is just a thumbnail sketch of some of the things we know about God from the picture he paints of himself in the Bible and that he hints at the very start of the Ten Commandments. It is just a tiny fraction of what could be said.

One night Saint Augustine had a dream in which he saw a little boy on a beach. The child was at the water's edge, scooping up the ocean in a thimble and pouring the water out onto the sand. In his dream Augustine heard an angel tell him that this boy would have emptied out the ocean long before anyone could possibly have exhausted what could be said about God.

All other gods are finite and will fail; they are not worth worshipping for a moment. Only the true and living God, God the creator, God the Lord, God the King and God the redeemer, is truly worthy of worship, and he is worth worshipping for eternity.

Getting right with God

The Commandments, then, are fundamentally about ensuring that we are in a right relationship with God and that we stay in it. As I come to the close of this book I want to spend some time focusing on just how we do that.

Recognize

Sometimes after a war or a power struggle in some country, we read that our government has "recognized" the new leadership. We need to do that with God.

First, recognize who God is. Many of us have an inadequate understanding of who God is. I have tried to explain something of the nature and character of the God who speaks to us in these commands. Can I challenge you to think about what you know of him? Maybe you now realize that you have had some inadequate idea of who God is and that it needs changing. Perhaps you need to admit, for the first time in your life, that God really does exist.

Second, recognize God's concern for you. The Bible tells the story of a God who cares for men and women even though they have rebelled against him. He cares for them so much that he has personally and painfully intervened in history in order to pay the price for their wrongdoings. He wants us to get into a right relationship with him. God desires us. He wants us to be friends with him, for us to know him in this life and throughout eternity, and for us to have abundant life. In short, he loves us.

Third, recognize God's demands. It is God who has given us these commands. He has given them to us because he made us, he knows what we are like, and he knows the best way for us to live. They are not given to become a weight around our neck but to give us boundaries within which we can live safely.

Fourth, recognize that God wants the fullest possible relationship with you. He wants first place in our lives, and he wants to rule over every area of who we are and what we are. There's sometimes a danger of thinking that God is just interested in the spiritual side of us. This is not the case. On a plane journey to the Atlanta Olympics a journalist asked President Clinton what his favorite event was. Without hesitation he said, "The decathlon." He went on to explain that this event, with its ten different sections, was so like life because there were separate disciplines which all had to be concentrated on with equal determination. Now, many people compartmentalize their lives. You hear people say that they are only able to cope in life because they live their life in separate compartments, such as work, home, family, friends, pleasure, hopes, and loyalties. These things can often be in watertight compartments that are kept entirely separate from one another.

The God of the Bible won't put up with being kept in a little compartment marked "spiritual." He isn't a one-day-a-week or a special-occasion God. In this first commandment, God spells out what he expects, which is everything. Let's face it, he deserves nothing less than that. God is God. He is not applying for a job or bargaining for a position. Giving God the number one spot in our lives is not us doing him a favor; it is simply us recognizing the position that is rightfully his.

Review

Having recognized all that God is and all that he demands of us, it is worth taking some time to do some stocktaking of our life as one of God's people. Let me remind you about some of the issues that we have looked at in this book.

Coveting. What is it that we aspire to? Who sets our desires? Do we desire what God desires or are we getting caught up in chasing after the things of this world? Do we trust him to provide all we need?

False testimony. Does the fact that God hears every word we say give us any cause to be ashamed? Are we truth tellers? Could we say that the words we use are always right? Is this an area of life in which we feel we have God and his standards at the center?

Stealing. Are there things that we have acquired through dishonest means? Are all our dealings in order and above board? Does our life speak of the honesty of God? Do we put God first in our finances?

Adultery. In our relationships with members of the opposite sex, is there ambiguity or secrecy? If we are married, are we faithful to our partner in all our actions, thoughts, and desires? Is our sexuality something we feel God is glorified by?

Murder. Are there people who we refuse to forgive? Are our relationships, at work and at home, healthy and free from malice and resentment? Are we prone to violence or harming another person in any way?

Honoring parents. Does our family life, whatever shape it takes, honor God? Is there respect and gratitude, commitment and care? If some of the people we work with or mix with could see us in our home environment, would they be surprised by how we treat those closest to us? Is God the head of our family?

Day of rest. Do we take regular time off each week? Do we trust God enough to take a whole day off? Do we use that time wisely? Is there anything we do with our time that we are ashamed of in front of God?

The name of God. Do we live consistently? Do we swear? Do we ever justify our ideas by saying that God is behind them? Do we bring honor to the name of God?

Idols. Are there things that have us in their grasp, such as money, sex, or power? Do we ever find ourselves controlled by desires we feel powerless to resist? Do we have divided loyalties? Does anything else claim the number one spot in our lives?

I don't know about you, but I barely get past the first of these before being challenged about what God wants for my life. None of us can keep the Ten Commandments. In fact there is only one person who has ever kept them, and his name is Jesus. It is because he was able to live a life that pleased God in every way that he was able to pay the price for our lives that fall short in so many ways. Falling short of what God requires of us is called sin—something we are all guilty of and, what's worse, unable to do anything about.

Fortunately, we are not left simply under the judgment of God. We may be those who have broken the Commandments, but God has intervened in Jesus to help us.

Respond

It is quite amazing that God, rather than leaving us in the dark to work out how best to live, gives us instructions so that we can be the people we were made to be. Far from despairing of us, God himself in Jesus comes and pays the penalty for our rebellion from him and his ways.

God does this because of his love for each one of us, not because we earn it or have to show ourselves worthy of it. We do, however, have to accept it. Admitting our wrongdoing, we must say yes to him and all that he has done for us. In grateful response to him we must now seek to put him first in everything. As he knows how weak we are, he fills us with his Holy Spirit so that we are able to do what he asks of us. It is only in the strength that the Holy Spirit gives that we can live lives that honor him.

It's easy to think that, even if we are forgiven, we are no more than God's servants. But in fact he wants us to be his friends and his children. So it isn't that he just wants us to do the right things; he wants us to have a right relationship with him.

What should characterize our relationship with God? Let me

suggest that, as in any friendship, time is needed. One of the ways we keep God at the center of our lives is to give him time. There is no better habit to develop than spending regular time with God. I would encourage you to carve out time, as busy as your schedule is, and set this time aside just to be face-to-face with him. During my face-to-face times with God I try to spend an equal proportion of the time in each of the following areas:

Praise. Give time to praising God, as a response to all he has done. This is one of the best antidotes to this generation's biggest problem, which is our obsession with ourselves. When we turn to God and put him at the center of our lives, we take the focus off ourselves and put it onto him. Focus on him—worshipping and thanking him for all he has done.

The Bible. Read his Word and listen to what he says. This takes the focus off listening to both our own words and all the advice and opinions in the world around us. Jesus himself said, "People do not live by bread alone, but by every word that comes from the mouth of God" (Matt. 4:4 NLT). There is very little to excuse how little we know of God's Word. A very godly man called John Henry Newman once said, "I read the newspaper to know what people are doing, and I read the Bible to know what people ought to be doing."

Confession. We must lay our lives open to him, asking him to show us where we haven't put him at the center, as well as times when we have lived in ways that have harmed our relationship, and ask for his forgiveness.

Prayer. We bring our needs and concerns to him and ask him to establish his ways in the world. Again this serves to help us take our hands off the things that it is so tempting to hold on to, and give them over to God.

These four things—praise, reading the Bible, confession, praying for ourselves and others—have been the main elements of time spent with God by Christians for two thousand years.

However, I need to say that being face-to-face with God isn't just an individual thing; it also involves others. The Bible leaves no doubt that God wants me to meet with other people who love his name. Attending church is not some optional extra that is only for Christians who are particularly sociable. Church is where we can meet with others who are seeking to live their lives completely for God, so that we can worship him together, learn more about him, remember his death with bread and wine, and seek together to serve the world about us, as well as celebrate his life among us. In such an environment of trust we can be open about how difficult it is sometimes. We all have blind spots, and other people can point out areas of our lives that we aren't aware of that are displeasing God. We can then receive support and advice.

It is more than likely that you know that the church isn't everything it should be. Perhaps you have had negative experiences of a local church or of Christians. But God is committed to his church, for the church is his people, and we must be too. If you are going to obey this first commandment, you must get involved in a church.

I want to conclude practically, by encouraging you to pray the following prayer. In some churches this prayer is prayed by the whole congregation at the beginning of each new year. It is a radical prayer of commitment to God, giving him everything and trusting him with all we are and all we have, from this day on. It is not a prayer that can be prayed lightly or flippantly. It is a prayer that changes our lives.

Holy God, I am no longer my own, but yours. Put me to what you will, rank me with whom you will; put me to doing, put me to suffering; let me be employed by you or laid aside for you, exalted for you or brought low for you; let me be full, let me be empty; let me have all things, let me have nothing; I freely and heartily yield all things to your pleasure and disposal.

And now, O glorious and blessed God, Father, Son and Holy Spirit, you are mine and I am yours. So be it. And the covenant that I have made on earth, let it be ratified in heaven. Amen.

To pray this is only possible because we know that the God we pray to knows us and loves us. Therefore, we can trust his promises and give ourselves to obeying his commands, relying on his endless forgiveness, grace, and strength.

> See, I set before you today life and prosperity, death and destruction. For I command you today to love the LORD your God, to walk in his ways, and to keep his commands, decrees and laws; then you will live and increase, and the LORD your God will bless you … (Deut. 30:15–16)

STUDY GUIDE

This guide is for individuals and groups who want to go deeper in this book through personal study and/or discussion. If you're studying with a group, the best way to use this guide is to read the chapter, work through the "On Your Own" questions yourself, then meet with your group to discuss what you learned. Some groups may prefer to have participants do just half a dozen or so questions on their own before the meeting in order to reduce prep time.

Some of the "On Your Own" questions ask you to examine your life, and if you're meeting with a group of people you don't know well, you might not want to share all the personal details. That's fine. For the first few chapters, this guide provides a separate section for groups to show how a group leader can select questions for discussion. That way, you can be completely honest with your self-examination on your own and then talk with your group at a level that seems appropriate. After the first few chapters, it should be clear which questions are good for your group to discuss.

There are generally more questions listed here than a group can dig into deeply in an hour or so, but that gives the leader the freedom to select topics that seem most helpful for the group. In the same way, if you're studying on your own, you can select the questions that point to areas you think God wants you to focus on.

TEN: YOU SHALL NOT COVET
On Your Own

1. Make a list of things you want that you don't have. Include material things, emotional ones, spiritual ones, whatever. Big, small. Possessions, experiences, people, lifestyle, personal traits, abilities.

2. The commandment speaks of coveting things you want that somebody else has. Look at your list and put an arrow next to every item on your list that somebody else has—either someone you know personally or someone you know of, perhaps through the media.

3. Does it bother you that other people have what you don't? Put an X by each item in your list about which you are bothered in this way.

4. How would you describe this feeling of being bothered? For instance, would you call it anger, sadness, anxiety, envy, competitiveness?

5. Choose a want from your list that you think about a lot. What do you think having it would give you?

6. We often want things that we think will give us security, respect, or status among other people, love that won't abandon us, feelings of ecstasy or joy, relief from boredom, or feelings of being successful or important. Think of something you coveted in the past and eventually got. Did it give you what it promised? If so, how long did that benefit last?

(Note: Most of us have coveted something at some time in our lives, and most of us have eventually gotten at least one of those things. If you can't think of a single time you got what you coveted, what do you think that says about you and your experience of life? For example, has this simply not been an area of sin in your life? Are you the kind of person who avoids wanting anything very much because the pain of disappointment has been too great to bear, or because you tend to be passive and let other people set the agenda? Have your wants universally been frustrated?)

7. Read James 4:1–2. To what extent does this passage mirror your experience—frustrated cravings leading to conflict? Or do your frustrated cravings lead more to depression, despair, numbness, or unhealthy coping habits? Or are you generally pretty good about taking your frustrated desires to God and letting him help you grow spiritually amid the disappointment?

8. How is coveting different from merely wanting something? You might check a dictionary.

9. Some people feel guilty for wanting even legitimate things. It's as if they're unworthy and should shrink to take up less space in the world. But suppressing desire into deadness isn't the alternative to coveting. God isn't asking us to deaden our souls so that we never long for anything. He wants us to long for the things he promises.

    Look at your list of wants. Which of them are covetous desires (things you shouldn't want, or that you want too much, or that you want in ways that lead to hurting yourself or others) and which are legitimate? Which are things God offers? Are any of them things he forbids? Which of them are things he thinks aren't very important in the scheme of things? Which things do you think you rate about as highly as Jesus would, and which do you rate higher than he would?

    Put a star beside any of your wants that you think are just fine to want in the way you want them.

10. Make a list of things you're grateful for.

11. Compare the length of this list to the length of the list of your wants. Any insights?

12. How easy is it for you to feel gratitude? What helps? What gets in the way?

13. Another way of dealing with desire is with hope. Hope is another kind of wanting what we don't have, looking forward to having

it. Read Romans 8:22–25, and notice the passionate intensity of the hope Paul speaks of.

How is hope different from covetousness? (For instance, how are the thoughts of a hopeful person different from those of a covetous one? How are the emotions different? The actions? Do we hope for different things than we covet?)

14. Ask God to help you desire what he promises. Take your list of wants to him. First offer to him the things on your list that you suspect he doesn't think would be good for you to have. Tell him how that makes you feel about him. How do you see God when you look at your wants?

If you have covetous desires, confess them to him.

Then offer to him the things you want that are right to want. Can you ask for them? What would a stance of hope involve?

In Your Group

Ideally, everyone will come to your group meeting having done the above exercises. If not, give them ten minutes to get as far as they can with questions 1 through 7 on their own. Assure them that they won't have to share the details of their answers with the group, so they can be completely honest with themselves.

The following discussion questions will let participants debrief their answers to the degree that they feel comfortable being frank with the group. Normally the group leader doesn't answer all the questions, but it can be helpful if the group leader is the first person to answer the first discussion question and makes an effort to be open about his or her failings.

- What did you learn about yourself from making and marking up your list of wants?

- From questions 4 through 8, select those for discussion that seem most helpful to explore more deeply.

- How does coveting someone's stuff affect your relationship with that person?

- Take a moment for everyone to do question 9 on their own if they haven't already done so. What do you learn about yourself from doing this?

- Discuss question 12.

- Discuss question 13.

- If you have more time, read Matthew 6:25–26. What encourages you to trust God? What moves you to have trouble trusting him?

- If you have time, talk about how a person goes about letting God shape his or her desires and attitudes.

- If you did question 14 on your own, talk about how it affected you.

- Pray together as question 14 describes. Ask God to help you desire what he promises. Thank him for the good things you have. Ask him to help you break free from covetousness and become more grateful and hopeful. Ask him for the things you desire that are good desires. Pray for the others in your group.

NINE: YOU SHALL NOT GIVE FALSE TESTIMONY
On Your Own

"All that is secret will eventually be brought into the open, and everything that is concealed will be brought to light and made known to all." (Luke 8:17 NLT).

1. Read Luke 8:17. How do you feel when you contemplate this statement? Why?

2. a. Read 1 John 1:5–10. What do you think it means to say that "God is light"?

    b. Walking in the light (1:7) doesn't mean sinless perfection. If it did, John wouldn't say people who walk in the light need to confess their sins (1:9). So, what does walking in the light mean?

c. If God is so open to forgiving our sins if we confess them, why is it often hard for us to admit we've done wrong?

3. Make a list of wrongs you've committed that you've never told anyone about. If it seems overwhelming to review your whole life, try looking at the past five years. You don't have to share this list with anybody, just use it as an opportunity to tell yourself the truth about yourself.

4. If it's hard for you to make that list, what gets in the way? What thoughts or feelings come to you? What excuses for not doing it come to mind?

5. Read John 18:37–38. Then imagine this: Jesus is in handcuffs, arrested by people who want to maintain their powerful positions and not let him rock the boat. They have taken him to you to pass judgment on him. If you free him, you are going to be in big trouble with people who have the power to ruin your reputation, threaten your career, and make your life miserable. He says to you what he said to Pilate (18:37).

What do you say to him? What does he say back? Write or imagine a dialogue between you and Jesus.

6. a. Think back over times you've talked about other people in the past month. When, if ever, have you shared negative information about someone or talked about him or her in a negative light? Make a list of names of those people. (Can't remember?

For one week, try paying attention to what you say and make a mental note when you talk about someone.)

b. Identify your feelings about each person you listed. Do you actively dislike that person? If so, why? Do you not care about him or her one way or the other?

c. Sometimes we gossip in order to impress the person we're talking to. Think about the people to whom you speak negatively about others. How interested are you in impressing them?

7. a. Make a list of promises you've made during the past year. These might be as simple as commitments to finish a task at work by a certain date or to meet someone somewhere. Maybe you said yes to do something at your church or for your family.

    b. Put a check mark beside promises you've kept.

    c. What does this exercise tell you about yourself?

8. a. Have you recently said yes to something and later wished you'd said no? If so, why did you say yes? What would have happened if you had said no?

    b. Did you follow through on the commitment? If not, why not?

9. a. How have others been affected when you failed to follow through on a commitment? Or when you gossiped about someone? Or when you shaded the truth about something in order to make yourself look better?

    b. Do you tend to minimize the harm done by such actions, or can you be honest with yourself about the harm?

10. What do you think about finding someone to hold you accountable in your private life? If it sounds like a good idea, who might that person be? If you don't like the idea, why not?

11. Deep down, do you believe God understands what you have been through in your past? Explain.

12. God offers his Holy Spirit to help you overcome your past. Do you want that help? If the answer is "Yes, but …" what is the "but"?

13. Confess to God your secrets and sins. Ask for His Spirit to help you overcome your habits of gossip, telling less than the truth, hiding from the truth, or failing to keep your word. Write a prayer to him.

In Your Group

- Questions 1 and 2 above are both good for discussion.

- You don't need to share your list from question 3 with

your group. But talk about what it was like to be that honest with yourself. Did you make the list or skip it? Why? What's the point of making a list like that?

- Think about how safe a place your group is for participants to tell the truth about themselves to each other. Can you trust the others not to gossip or look down on you if you are honest? Or do you sense that others are pretending and expect you to do the same?

- Now discuss: What would make your group a safer place to be honest about yourself—maybe not to tell every last detail of your faults, but to be basically truthful about your struggles, the gaps in your faith, your failures to love others well, and so on?

- One thing that helps make a group safe is clear ground rules, such as:
  - *Confidentiality:* What is said in the group stays in the group.
  - *Attendance:* Participants make group meetings a priority, so there's continuity and people get to know each other over time.
  - *Respect:* No cutting remarks or put-downs.
  - *Advice:* Advice isn't given unless a person asks for it. Participants don't try to fix each other. They listen, ask questions, offer feedback, but don't tell each other what to do.

If your group doesn't already have clear ground rules, what ground rules would be good for your group?

- If you used questions 6 through 9 above to examine your life, what did you learn about yourself?
- Discuss questions 10 through 12.
- Give all the groups' members an opportunity to share one area of their life that they would like the group to pray about. (This should be about their life, not a friend's.) Pray for each other.

EIGHT: YOU SHALL NOT STEAL
On Your Own

1. Have you stolen anything in the past five years or so? If yes, then make a list of ways you have done that. Think about books borrowed but not returned, taxes evaded, supplies and time at work. Nobody is going to see this list but you and God, and God already knows it, so this is for you.

2. What did you learn about yourself? Were you surprised or not? Why? What are your weak areas?

3. Do you make justifications for thefts? If so, what are they?

4. What might you do to make amends for thefts?

5. What would it cost you in terms of time and money to steal absolutely nothing at work—no photocopies, pens, phone calls, time, etc.?

6. a. Read Matthew 6:19–21. Where is your treasure? What are you investing time and energy in?

   b. How is that affecting your heart?

7. a. Where does giving currently fit into your life?

   b. What would happen if you gave a tenth of your income to God's work in the world? (One-tenth isn't a biblical law, but it's a place to begin the conversation.)

   c. If there's an area of your life (money, possessions, time) in which you are most tempted to steal, that's a good area in which to give away more. As you search your heart, does it speak to you about some particular area?

8. a. What would relying on God for material things look like for you? What changes in attitude and actions would that involve?

   b. What help do you need to do this?

9. Slavery around the world, debt in developing countries, environmental stewardship. What do these have to do with you?

You can't do everything, but what is yours to do? Talk with God about this.

10. Employers generally tell themselves they're not underpaying their employees if they're paying them roughly what other employers pay them. What are the pros and cons of this as a standard for deciding what is right to pay workers?

In Your Group

- What did you learn about yourself from questions 1 through 5?
- Discuss questions 6 through 10, as much as you have time.
- Pair up with a partner and pray for each other about anything for which God has been convicting you.

SEVEN: YOU SHALL NOT COMMIT ADULTERY
On Your Own

1. If you're married, evaluate your marriage for the qualities described in this chapter. For instance:
    - Would you say your marriage shows a wholesale commitment, with no area where you hold back from surrendering to each other?
    - How are you doing at respect?
    - At behaving in a trustworthy way?
    - At taking responsibility for your faults and your actions?
    - At taking time to talk and listen?
    - At romance?

2. a. If you're single, what do you need from the Christian com-
    munity in order to maintain celibacy without loneliness?

    b. If you're married, how can you reach out to single people?

3. a. The Song of Songs is a collection of poems in which the voices
    go back and forth among a woman, her lover/fiancé, and her
    friends. For a sampling, read Song of Songs 4:9—5:1 and 7:7–10.
    How does the author depict erotic love?

    b. What impression do you get of the author's attitude toward
    sex?

    c. What do you think this is doing in the Bible? (For instance,
    do you think it's strictly an allegory of God's love for us? If
    so, what does it say about God that he uses sexual imagery to
    describe his love? If you think it's also about love between a man
    and a woman, what does that say about God?)

4. a. Read Song of Songs 8:6–7. This is probably the woman speak-
    ing to the man. She says real love is as strong as death, and she
    even links it with jealousy. Why is she so insistent about her
    lover being faithful to her?

    b. Is her attitude appropriate, in your view? Explain. (You might
    refer to the chapter for context.)

5. a. The Song of Songs presents two intense human longings: for passionate, sensual love and for committed love. Do you long for one of these? Both? Neither?

    b. Is it realistic to want both? Do you think most women you know long for both of these? What about most men you know?

6. The rest of the Old Testament presents a dismal collection of stories in which men and women fall far short of the picture of sexuality as it was meant to be that we get in Genesis 2 and the Song of Songs. The Old Testament portrays rape, incest, adultery that leads to murder, polygamy that leads to jealousy between wives, a king's harem of hundreds of women that pulls Israel into idolatry, marriages that start with love but turn bitter, prostitution, the brutal murder of a concubine—and on and on.

    What might God be saying to us by describing both the ideal and the worst of human sexuality, and then sending Jesus?

7. a. What do you think God would say to a person who wants the kind of sensual passion the Song of Songs depicts but isn't willing to commit to one partner for life?

    b. Children, busy careers, and sometimes boredom or unresolved conflict can drain a couple's energy for each other. What do you think God would say to a person who wants a committed marriage but has lost (or never had) the sexual passion the Song of Songs depicts?

8. Read Matthew 5:28. What does it mean to look at someone lustfully? How can you tell the difference between appreciating a person's beauty and lusting to possess them physically?

9. a. As you look at your own sexual past and present, what do you need from Jesus? Ask him for it.

   b. What action do you need to take? (For example, guarding your mind from sexually provocative input and thoughts, breaking off an inappropriate relationship, mending or making a firm commitment to a relationship, treating your spouse differently, seeking professional counseling.)

10. Pray Psalm 51 for yourself. Pray also to deeply know God's love for yourself—his passionate, faithful love that transcends anything you've done.

In Your Group

- Select from the above questions for discussion.
- Sometimes it's more appropriate to be honest about sexual matters in single-gender groups, and sometimes it's helpful to hear what the opposite sex has to say. If you're meeting in a mixed-gender group, you might want to discuss some of this chapter's questions all together (such as questions 3 through 8), then separate men from women for a time

in which participants can ask for prayer about themselves and/or their marriages (questions 1, 2, 9, 10). Appoint a leader for each subgroup who will guide this conversation away from griping about spouses and toward a focus on one's own need for God's help.

SIX: YOU SHALL NOT MURDER
On Your Own

1. Read Matthew 5:21–22. Why does Jesus treat anger as so serious, on a level with murder?

2. Which style of handling anger sounds most like you—the maniac, the mute, the martyr, or the manipulator? Describe what you do (or don't do) with anger.

3. What effect does your style of handling anger have on other people? On you?

4. a. What do you learn from Matthew 5:21–24 and Ephesians 4:26–27, 29–32 about how God wants you to handle your anger?

   b. How can you become a person who deals with anger like that?

   c. What help do you need from God? From other people?

"The problem with some people is that they think so little of themselves that they think they are always in the wrong. The problem with others is that they are so proud that they get angry because they think they are always right."

5. Which of the above problems sounds more like you, if either?

6. a. Is there anyone you need to forgive? Whom?

    b. What, if anything, hinders you from forgiving that person? (Forgiveness doesn't mean saying that what the person did was okay or didn't matter. It's letting go of the grudge and the longing for revenge.)

7. a. The chapter lists three reasons why human life is sacred. Which do you agree with, or which not?

    b. How is the sacredness of human life relevant to abortion? To euthanasia?

    c. Do you think there's a point at which life isn't worth living? If so, by what standards do we set such a point? If not, why not?

8. a. Do you believe that we can break the commandment about murder by simply doing nothing for those who are dying? Explain your view.

    b. What should you do for those who are at risk of dying of poverty?

9. a. God forgave Moses, David, and Paul for committing murder, and he did important work through them. For what do you need God's forgiveness?

    b. Do you ever doubt whether God can work through you because of things you've done? If so, what do you think God wants you to do with those doubts?

10. Write a prayer to God confessing your faults and asking for help in areas surfaced by this study.

In Your Group
- Select from the above questions for discussion.

FIVE: HONOR YOUR FATHER AND MOTHER

1. Describe your relationship with your parents, if they are alive. What are the positives and negatives? If you have no relationship, talk about why not.

2. What are your emotions toward your parents? Affection? Frustration? Gratitude? Anger? Fear? Disappointment? Grief? Joy? Indifference?

3. Why do they deserve your respect? (Or if you think they don't, say why.)

4. Why do you suppose the commandment links honoring parents to prospering as a person?

5.   How can you treat your parents with value and respect? How can you express appreciation, involve them in your life, or in other ways honor them? (If one or both of them has harmed you or someone close to you in the past, how can you treat them with respect without letting them inflict harm? For example, some people always take a friend or spouse with them to visit a parent who is likely to be insulting in one-on-one visits.)

6.   a. Have your parents done anything that you find it hard to forgive? If so, what?

     b. Forgiveness doesn't mean minimizing the harm. Nor does it mean putting yourself or others in a situation where the harm can be repeated. Talk with God about what it might mean to forgive your parents. You might also want to talk with one or more trusted friends and ask them to pray with you.

7.   How is God a good parent to you?

8.   Are you unhappy or uncomfortable with God as your parent? If thinking of him as your parent seems negative to you, or if you feel he has let you down, talk about why.

9.   If you're a parent, think about how much time you give to your children and how much time you put into listening to them and communicating openly with them. By your actions, how high a priority are you putting on your children, compared to other things?

10. a. What are your strengths as a parent?

    b. What are your weaknesses?

11. How can you discipline your children appropriately?

12. What could you do to earn your children's respect and trust (not necessarily their total approval, as parenting isn't a popularity contest, but their trust)?

13. a. As a parent, what do you need from the Holy Spirit? Ask him.

    b. What do you need from Christian friends?

14. God is a perfect parent, yet the Bible shows how endlessly rebellious and disrespectful his children are. Does it help you to know that God understands how painful it can be to be a parent? What do you want to say to him about this?

In Your Group
  • Select from the above questions for discussion.

FOUR: REMEMBER THE SABBATH DAY

1. How many hours of sleep do you get each night, on average?

2. Do you take a day each week to rest? If so, what do you generally do on that day? If not, why not?

3. Do you feel you get enough rest? If not, what gets in the way? How long has your life lacked rest?

4. Do you feel guilty or anxious when you aren't doing something productive? If so, why?

5. If someone were to look at your current pattern of work and rest, who or what would they say runs your life? Explain.

6. How would resting make a statement about who runs your life?

7. Why does God have to command us to take a break? Why don't we do it of our own free will?

8. What evidence do you have to think that God can be trusted to provide for you even if you take a day off? Do you have evidence to the contrary?

9. What might Sabbath look like for a parent of small children, given that toddlers need to be fed, bathed, and attended to every day, virtually all day?

10. How can you guard your rest? How can you make sure your day of rest is truly restful and life-giving, rather than stressful? Think of practical steps to take.

11. When does God have an opportunity to look into your heart?

12. How can you stand up for others' right to rest? Is there anything you currently do that hinders others from doing this? How does this work in a pluralistic society, where not everybody is Christian and wants to rest on a Sunday, and where so many people want to shop on Sundays because they work the other days of the week?

13. a. Write a list of reasons to be thankful for your work.

    b. Do you have another inner voice that says something very different about your work? If so, what does it say? Do you think that voice would complain about all work, or is your current job a problem that you need to address?

14. Where do you see God's good design in your work? How does your work benefit others? (Maybe you produce a product or service that benefits people. Or if you feel your work contributes nothing useful, is there something else you could do that would be of value?)

15. Read Colossians 3:23–24. Do you do your work for God? If so, how does doing so make a difference to the way you work or to what goes on inside you while you work? If not, what would shifting to working for God involve?

16. How does our society define a "fulfilling" job? How might God's idea of a fulfilling job be different?

In Your Group
- Select from the above questions for discussion.

THREE: YOU SHALL NOT MISUSE THE NAME OF THE LORD

1. How does it matter to you that God is YHWH?

2. a. Have you experienced Jesus as Savior (God for you) and Immanuel (God with you)? If so, how?

   b. Is he these things for you now, or has your awareness of him as rescuer and present with you dimmed? If the latter, how did that happen?

3. a. What are you saying when you call God "Our Father" or even "Abba"?

   b. How can you live out this intimacy?

4. a. What are you saying when you say, "may your name be honored"?

   b. How can you go about honoring his name?

5. Which is harder for you: the intimate familiarity, or the honor and respect? Why?

6. What has God done that is worthy of your respect?

7. Some people believe God made and sustains the universe, but they take it for granted and don't treat him with much respect. Why do you suppose that's so common?

8. a. What power does God's name have?

    b. How does it affect a person's life to truly believe God's name has power?

    c. Do Christians ever use God's name as if it were magic, as if it were a power they controlled? If so, how?

9. Many people doubt God's perfect character and suspect him of the same kinds of selfishness and injustice that human authorities are so often guilty of. Do you have a nagging voice that suspects God like that? Have you had experiences that make you fear he may be unfair or indifferent? If so, talk those out with him. Is there anybody you can talk to honestly about this?

10. Can you think of any recent situations when God's name or Christianity have been used to oppress, intimidate, hurt, or exploit others? If so, explain.

11. Have you ever used God's name to make yourself look good or to further your own projects? If so, how?

12. Reflect on your attitude at a recent worship service. Do you go to get something out of it or to give something to God? What would the latter involve?

13. Make a list of things you count as your achievements. Have you ever thanked God for them? Do you feel that in these areas you have given him the honor that's due to him? Thank him now for each item. How does doing this affect you?

14. How can you tell a God-centered prayer from a self-centered one?

15. Write a God-centered prayer. Call on him by name.

In Your Group

• Select from the above questions for discussion.

TWO: YOU SHALL NOT MAKE FOR YOURSELF AN IDOL
On Your Own

1. In the following sentences, what would you put in the place of the word *God?* (Examples: money, my career, my family, possessions, what people think of me, my body, sports, music, sex, power/control.) Be honest; this is just between you and God.

   • God gives purpose, meaning and fulfillment to my life.
   • God governs the way I act.
   • God is the focal point around which my existence hangs.

- God is often in my thoughts, and I get enthusiastic about God.
- Thoughts of God comfort me when I am down.
- I read about God, I talk about God, I make friends with those who are also committed to God.
- I desire more of God.

2. Are the things you're tempted to put in God's place basically good things that you blow out of proportion? If so, how does their goodness make the idolatry more appealing?

3. Do the things you're tempted to put in God's place make fewer moral demands on you than the real God does? If so, explain how.

4. a. What do these tempting idols promise to give you if you worship them?

   b. What, if anything, have they delivered?

5. Idols often make few moral demands, but they do make demands. What sacrifices in terms of time, money, attention, good relationships, shame, fear, or other losses has idolatry cost you?

6. How do you respond to the idea that your relationship with God is like a marriage, and your longing for other things ahead of God is like infidelity?

7. Do you resist the idea of marital commitment to God, prefer-
    ring to date him and other gods as well? If so, why is staying
    committed to God so hard?

8. Choose one or more of the idols of our time listed in this chapter:
    sex, the environment, the human body, power, or possessions.

    a. Have you been tempted to worship that? If so, how has it
    appealed to you? How have your thoughts and actions been
    affected?

    b. How can we go about reclaiming that good thing for God?

    c. How can we help others who are pursuing this thing in an
    idolatrous way?

9. What is a reasonable, nonidolatrous amount of time and money
    for you to devote to your physical appearance?

10. What would God like you to do for the care of the natural
    world?

11. a. Read John 18:28—19:16. Who in this story worships power?
    How can you tell?

    b. How does Jesus use power in this story?

    c. What can we learn from Jesus about power?

12. How has idolatry harmed you?

13. When people worship idols they become like them: more and more unreal, more and more untrue, more and more false, and more and more dead. Can you see any signs of that in your own life? If so, what are they?

14. Give some examples of how we can treat God as an idol, at our beck and call to fulfill our desires or agendas.

15. a. After this study of idols, what is God calling you to do?

    b. What help do you need?

In Your Group

- Select from the above questions for discussion. Some groups may be intimate enough to confess their idols to one another. Other groups may prefer to talk about their experience of idolatry without naming their most socially taboo idols (such as sex). It's a good idea to have at least one person of the same gender to whom you can name your idols and exactly what you've done to worship them, but mixed-gender groups aren't always good settings to talk frankly about Internet pornography, for example. Group leaders should set an example by being open, yet appropriate, about their weaknesses.
- Consider dividing into smaller subgroups for prayer.

ONE: YOU SHALL HAVE NO OTHER GODS
On Your Own

1. a. Read Isaiah 40:21–26. How does Isaiah describe God?

    b. Read the passage slowly again. At each sentence, ask yourself, "How does this apply to me?"

    c. Pray the passage back to God. Sentence by sentence, perhaps rephrasing it in your own words, say, "Lord, you ..."

2. Some people believe in a God that is an impersonal force. They might even say that Isaiah's language about God, which envisions him as a person, is just poetry. Why does it matter whether God is a person or an impersonal spirit?

3. a. In Colossians 1:15–20, Paul describes Jesus (a particular human being whose physical blood was shed) as the universe's Creator and Sustainer.

    b. What is extraordinary about this? Why does it matter?

4. Has God revealed himself to you? Is he allowing you to find him? Explain.

5. a. In Jesus, we see what God is really like. For instance, what does Mark 1:40–42 reveal about God?

b. When you put this picture of God side by side with what Isaiah 40:21–26 says, what impression of God do you get?

6. a. If a person accepts Jesus as King, what are the implications?

b. How do you feel about the implications for you personally?

7. Describe the slavery from which God has rescued you (or from which he could rescue you if you decide to let him).

8. a. Which of these do you need to recognize more deeply than you do now?
    - Who God is
    - God's concern for you
    - God's demands
    - God's desire for first place in your life

b. What action do you need to take to recognize these things? What help do you need?

9. For what are you grateful in this study? Take some time to thank God and to worship him for who he is.

In Your Group

- Select from the above questions for discussion.
- Take time to thank God for your group and to worship him for who he is. Tell him how this group has affected you.

BIBLIOGRAPHY

Bass, Dorothy, "Keeping Sabbath" in *Practising Our Faith* (San Francisco: Jossey-Bass, 1997).

Bloomfield, Harold H. with Leonard Felder, *Making Peace With Your Parents* (New York: Ballantine Books, 1996).

Carson, D. A., R. T. France, J. A. Motyer and G. J. Wenham (eds), *New Bible Commentary* (Leicester: IVP, 1994).

Cole, R. A., *Exodus* (Leicester: IVP, 1973).

Craigie, P. C., "The Ten Commandments" in Walter A. Elwell (ed.), *Evangelical Dictionary of Theology* (London: Marshall Pickering, 1985).

Cray, Graham, *Postmodern Culture and Youth Discipleship* (Cambridge: Grove Books, 1999).

Edwards, Brian H., *The Ten Commandments for Today* (Bromley: Day One Publications, 1996).

Felder, Leonard, *The Ten Challenges* (New York: Harmony Books, 1997).

Field, David, *God's Good Life: The Ten Commandments for the 21st Century* (Leicester: IVP, 1992).

Ford, David F., *The Shape of Living* (London: HarperCollins, 1997). 291

Harrelson, Walter, "Ten Commandments," in Bruce M. Metzger and Michael D. Coogan (eds), *The Oxford Companion to the Bible* (Oxford: Oxford University Press, 1993).

Horton, Michael S., *The Law of Perfect Freedom* (Chicago: Moody Press, 1999).

Kaiser, W., "Exodus" in *Expositor's Bible Commentary* (Michigan: Zondervan, 1990).

Kendall, R. T., *Just Grace* (London: SPCK, 2000).

Kline, M. G., "Ten Commandments" in *The Illustrated Bible Dictionary*, 1st ed. (Leicester: IVP, 1980).

MacDonald, Gordon, *Ordering Your Private World* (Crowborough: Highland, 1987).

McCarthy, John, *Some Other Rainbow* (London: BCA, 1993).

Mehl, Ron, *The Ten(der) Commandments* (Oregon: Multnomah Publishers, 1998).

Schlessinger, Laura, *The Ten Commandments* (New York: HarperCollins, 1998).

Sider, Ronald J., *Rich Christians in an Age of Hunger* (London: Hodder & Stoughton, 1990).

Sine, Tom, *Mustard Seed Versus McWorld* (London: Monarch, 1990).

Storkey, Elaine, *The Search for Intimacy* (London: Hodder & Stoughton, 1995).

Volf, Miroslav, *Exclusion and Embrace* (Nashville: Abingdon, 1996).

Wright, N. T., *Following Jesus* (London: SPCK 1993).

Wright, N. T., *New Tasks for a Renewed Church* (London: Hodder & Stoughton, 1992).

ABOUT THE AUTHOR

J.John, a Greek-Cypriot by birth, lives in Chorleywood, England. He is married to Killy, and they have three sons, Michael, Simeon, and Benjamin. J.John became a Christian in 1975. J.John has been described as refreshing, humorous, passionate, earthy, accessible, and dynamic.

J.John is regarded as one of the most creative Christian speakers with an appeal that transcends gender, age, race, culture, and occupation. His much-loved art of storytelling helps people discover spiritual meaning in a way that makes sense of everyday life.

For further information on J.John, visit www.philotrust.com